Think
In Defence of a Thoughtful Life

Svend Brinkmann

Translated by Tam McTurk

polity

Originally published in Danish as Tænk © Svend Brinkmann & Gyldendal, Copenhagen, 2022. Published by agreement with Gyldendal Group Agency.

This English edition © Polity Press, 2024

Translated by Tam McTurk

The publisher gratefully acknowledges the assistance given by the Danish Arts Foundation towards the translation of this book.

Polity Press
65 Bridge Street
Cambridge CB2 1UR, UK

Polity Press
111 River Street
Hoboken, NJ 07030, USA

All rights reserved. Except for the quotation of short passages for the purpose of criticism and review, no part of this publication may be reproduced, stored in a retrieval system or transmitted, in any form or by any means, electronic, mechanical, photocopying, recording or otherwise, without the prior permission of the publisher.

ISBN-13: 978-1-5095-5958-9
ISBN-13: 978-1-5095-5959-6 (pb)

A catalogue record for this book is available from the British Library.

Library of Congress Control Number: 2023934524

Typeset in 11 on 14 pt Fournier by
Cheshire Typesetting Ltd, Cuddington, Cheshire
Printed and bound by CPI Group (UK) Ltd, Croydon, CR0 4YY

The publisher has used its best endeavours to ensure that the URLs for external websites referred to in this book are correct and active at the time of going to press. However, the publisher has no responsibility for the websites and can make no guarantee that a site will remain live or that the content is or will remain appropriate.

Every effort has been made to trace all copyright holders, but if any have been overlooked the publisher will be pleased to include any necessary credits in any subsequent reprint or edition.

For further information on Polity, visit our website:
politybooks.com

Contents

Introduction		1
1	What do you think?	13
2	Why has it become difficult to think?	29
3	Happiness is a thoughtful life	55
4	Thinking as formation	68
5	Where does thinking come from?	91
6	How to think	106
Notes		119

Introduction

Some years ago, I wrote a review of the excellent book *Thinking, Fast and Slow* by Daniel Kahneman, the renowned psychologist and winner of the Nobel Prize in Economics (there is no prize for psychology).[1] As the title suggests, the book is about how human thought operates via two systems: a fast one, which is intuitive and usually quite effective, but also has an inbuilt tendency to make mistakes; and a slow one that is more mentally demanding but often more reliable. In my review, I cited one of Kahneman's well-known examples, which I have reproduced below. When you read it, try to blurt out your answer to the simple sum automatically – and then wait for a minute or two before working it out systematically.

> A bat and ball cost $1.10.
> The bat costs one dollar more than the ball.
> How much does the ball cost?

Easy enough, you might think. Most people's quick-fire intuitive answer is 10 cents. Indeed, that may be how it looks at first glance, but think a little deeper and longer and you'll realise it's wrong. If the ball costs 10 cents and the bat costs a dollar more than the ball, the bat must cost $1.10, which takes the total cost above the amount stipulated in the original premise. The correct answer must be that the ball costs 5 cents (and the bat $1.05). Elementary arithmetic, perhaps, but not immediately obvious to the fast thinker – even for gifted adults like you, the reader. As the example shows, following your intuition or gut feeling isn't always the best way to go. For some questions and problems, it's better to slow down. The first thing that springs to mind isn't always right, no matter how many people claim otherwise, including the authors of self-help books and management manuals.

I cite this example not just because it is an exemplary illustration of one of the kinds of cognitive errors that Kahneman has spent a long career studying, but also because, after reading my review, an angry woman – a complete stranger – called me about it. She sounded rational enough and wanted to take me to task for what she considered a self-evident mistake. It was clear to all and sundry that the ball cost 10 cents! She sounded almost embarrassed on my behalf because I didn't get it. I tried to be patient and talk her through the sum, but she stood firm. (I may have written a book about standing firm, but this wasn't really what I had in mind!)

My critic passionately explained why I was wrong. Getting me to think straight obviously meant a great deal to her. My failure (in her eyes) to grasp the problem bothered her, and she wanted to help. Her concern echoed Kahneman's desire to help his readers think better and train them to minimise cognitive errors. For most of us, it's important not only that we and our fellow human beings *behave* properly – comply with certain *moral virtues* – but also that we *think* properly and, in doing so, comply with certain *intellectual virtues*. It's important not only to *act well* but also to *think well*. Doing so puts us in touch with reality, which helps us learn. It also encourages us to think critically, which allows us to identify those aspects of the world in need of improvement. Good, deep thinking can also be – in my opinion – a source of true joy. Especially when we *think for ourselves*. The ancient Greek philosophers lauded the joy of thinking, of thoughtfulness, of the contemplative life, and considered it the highest human calling. That is what this book is all about – advocating a thoughtful life.

The difference between Kahneman and the woman on the phone, of course, is that one is right and the other wrong. There is only one correct answer to a sum. All others are wrong. This underlines the fundamental normativity of thinking: that there are more or less correct ways to deploy our capacity to think. There are, quite simply, norms for good and valid thinking, and we would do well to learn them. One theme of this book is that learning to think is part of the process known as formation (*Bildung*, as the Germans call it) – learning to be a fully rounded thinking person – which is described in detail later in the book. Thinking is fundamental to living a good life.

To the best of our knowledge, humans are the only creatures on the planet capable of thinking in the true sense of the word. All sorts of animals intuitively calculate risk (a hyena tempted to steal from a lion weighs up the risk of finding themselves on the menu), but only humans make actual calculations, because only we have access to the world of numbers and mathematical symbols. Humans are also the only creatures capable of thinking about the meaning of life, the nature of a just society or the potential existence of a deity. We can do these things because we possess the ability to think reflectively – to think about how we think – and because we have language, which the philosopher Ludwig Wittgenstein called 'the vehicle of thought'.[2] We need language and its concepts in order to think about the past, the future, good, evil, or other abstract matters, including thinking itself.

However, even though thinking is normative – that is, it can be right and wrong – and even though some of its norms appear objective (those of logic, for example), it's still important that we learn to think for ourselves. The rounded individual understands the history and communities of which they are a part, and can think independently. They have developed their own voice, which makes them capable of forming their own opinions about issues and questions, but when doing so they always take into account other people and the world around them. Indeed, this is the basic idea of humanism: that you must learn to think for yourself. To think well. To use your reason. And to resist anything that threatens your ability to do so. But how do we manage that as products of our circumstances? How can we think slowly, deeply and in a rounded manner in a world driven by utility value, power and haste? These are the type of questions addressed in this book. I will argue that thinking, in the true sense of the word, is one of the most important things you can do in life – and one of the most human things, too. However, I will also assert that the nature of our modern world is not conducive to thoughtfulness, and that this means there is every reason for us to re-learn how to think well and deeply.

Why practise something you already know how to do?

We live in strange times. Although most of us are perfectly capable of using our legs to go for a walk, books about how to walk and hike are published all the time. The majority of us manage to fall asleep most nights, yet a torrent of literature is churned out about how to sleep better. And even though many people know what it feels like to fall into a reverie and just be there in the moment, bookshop shelves are bulging with guides to meditation and mindfulness, which treat the phenomenon as a technique to be taught. Humans really are uniquely capable of making their own bodies and minds the object of training, discipline and improvement. We are, as the German philosopher Peter Sloterdijk puts it, creatures condemned to practise even the most simple and uncomplicated of things.

It is easy to marvel and poke fun at this 'technification' of the simple – I should know, and readily admit that I have been guilty of doing just that. Nevertheless, I intend to stick my neck out in this book and add yet another area to the list of phenomena that we all already know about and yet, I maintain, a lot of us would do well to practise: thinking.

But what is thinking? It is clearly more than just solving mathematical problems, as in Kahneman's example. Can we arrive at a tentative understanding of the phenomenon even at this early stage in the book?

Before I introduce definitions and theories about thinking, let me hark back to some of the most delightful moments I can remember, moments that revolved around precisely that – thinking. As a child, I would spend hours lying on the carpet, basking in the spring sun as it flooded in through our big living room windows, just letting my mind wander. In my head, I told myself stories and dreamt of being an explorer. Sometimes, an atlas would help kickstart my imagination. This was thinking as joyful daydreaming. In the winter, this form of reverie would take place in front of the wood-burning stove, and it's surely no coincidence that I often fell into thought as the sun or the wood burner warmed my body. Often, my thinking was accompanied by distinct physical sensations. For example, I would feel a bit faint or empty when I pondered whether the universe is infinite. Neither finiteness nor infinity is comprehensible, yet the question is worth thinking about. As I walked the few miles to school, I often conducted long conversations with myself which – unlike my physical being – had no particular destination. It was probably the very absence of ulterior goals that made the thinking so edifying. It was thinking just for the sake of thinking. I also remember the embarrassment of occasionally being caught talking to myself as I ambled along, lost in thought. These days, I know there was nothing to be ashamed of – I was just deeply immersed in my thoughts.

As an adult, I find it more difficult to lose myself in thought like that, but it still happens sometimes when I'm out for a run or a bike ride. Often, it results in useful ideas that I write down when I get home. But I can't just make this happen whenever I feel like it. Thinking has a life of its own. You can't do much more than listen to your thoughts. They are, of course, *my* thoughts – I think them *myself* – and yet I don't really know where they come from (well, from the brain, of course, but not just from there, as we will see later). In a way, it's as much the thinking that is thinking through me as it is me who is doing the thinking. It's almost like being a spectator to the world of ideas, which plays out inside you – or even outside you, for example if you write thoughts down or discuss them with others. I don't have control over what pops up once I start thinking, but I can listen to the flow, try to keep up and take part in the dialogue with myself. In ancient philosophy, Socrates, in particular, was known for long bouts of reverie, when what he called his *daimon* – his inner voice – spoke to him through his thoughts. Fortunately, the world-famous wise man is not the only one with such a *daimon*. We all have one. Children are especially good at giving free rein to theirs. In fact, the ancient Greek concept of the good life, *eudaimonia*, stems from *eudaimon*, which literally means 'good *daimon*'.

My thesis in this book is that more thinking would enrich our lives. We ought to listen more to our *daimon*. In our busy, modern existence, there's often no time for forethought, consideration and afterthought – all of which depend, in many ways, on our *daimon*, which makes itself heard when we allow ourselves the time to dwell a little on our thoughts, to be conscientious and think critically. Spending time with your thoughts, letting them wander freely with no particular destination, marvelling at the world, immersing yourself in life's mysteries, and insisting on time for both anticipation and reflection are all aspects of what I call thoughtfulness. If you miss thinking as much as I do, you'll be glad to hear that you can reawaken your *daimon*. That's the aim of this book.

Introduction

The thinking human

It's difficult to come up with a more fundamental human phenomenon than the capacity to think. Our biological species is even called *homo sapiens* – Latin for 'wise man' or 'thinking human'. The entire tradition of European philosophy has stressed the importance of *rational* thinking. In ancient Greece, Aristotle defined human beings as *zoon logikon*, the rational animal. During the Enlightenment, Immanuel Kant stressed that the capacity for rationality is fundamental to human dignity and to being human. Animals are different. They can't relate to themselves, use language or assume responsibilities, all of which are traits linked to the ability to think. Kant is famous for (among other things) his 1784 description of enlightenment as 'man's emergence from his self-imposed nonage'. He defined *nonage* as 'the inability to use one's own understanding without another's guidance'. In other words, nonage is self-inflicted when it stems not from any lack of intellect but from a lack of decisiveness and the courage to deploy the ability to think. Hence Kant's Enlightenment slogan *Sapere aude!* ('have the courage to use your own reason'). Think for yourself, we might also say. Listen to your *daimon*. Talk with it and with other people.

The point is that we can all think for ourselves if we so wish, but deciding to do so requires courage. 'Self-imposed nonage' is often easier. The philosopher Hannah Arendt argued that this was what the Nazi war criminal Adolf Eichmann did as part of the apparatus that orchestrated the Holocaust – the systematic extermination of the Jewish people – and the mass murder of others who thought differently from the regime. Arendt concluded that Eichmann's fundamental defect was his inability to think. There is always a danger that unthinking people will act in an evil manner. We will return to that.

What does thinking mean?

But what does it actually mean to think? What forms does it take? How do you learn to do it? And how easy or difficult is it to think for yourself these days?

These are some of the questions this book attempts to answer. In doing so, I draw on psychology – especially the cognitive strand that focuses on how we think and understand – but also philosophy, because my primary interest is in what might be called the existential dimensions of thinking. The idea is that thinking isn't just a matter of solving intellectual problems, like Kahneman's tricky sum. It can also be a way of existing in the world – living a contemplative life.

Social scientists and philosophers have long identified a lack of thinking in contemporary society. More than seventy years ago, the existential philosopher and cultural critic Martin Heidegger declared that 'What is most thought-provoking in our thought-provoking time is that we are still not thinking.'[3] He meant it not just as a critique of his own age, but as a more general analysis of the tendency to avoid thinking that had characterised more or less the whole of Western cultural history. According to Heidegger, we have simply forgotten to think, in the sense of thinking for its own sake. Since Heidegger, we have become even better at using science and technology to solve myriad problems. This calls for a great deal of cognitive activity, of course, which we seek to stimulate in kindergartens, schools, and in further and higher education. As a society, we like to focus on utilitarian thinking – on 'what works', effectiveness and evidence, and 'the biggest bang for our buck'. It is, of course, legitimate to think instrumentally in this way. But what if, in doing so, we forget the intrinsic value of letting our thoughts wander, and of allowing them to lead us to unforeseen destinations? There is much to be gained by spending time thinking thoughts that are not of any immediate use – thoughts about life, the universe and what makes a society just. We can do this on our own or as part of dynamic conversations with others. It is often in situations like these that we think critically and open our minds to the possibility that things could be different. Who decided the world should be as it is? Could it be better?

I call this form of thinking – which has no ulterior motive, making it both the finest and least practical form – *thoughtfulness*. This is what I advocate in this book. It is the form of thinking closest to meaningfulness. Given the burgeoning popularity of mindfulness in recent decades, I hope thoughtfulness will be just as popular one day. Mindfulness means 'being present in the here and now and accepting what is',[4] and it builds on the meditative traditions of the Far East. Studies of the therapeutic effects of mindfulness indicate promising outcomes in the treatment of stress, anxiety and depression. Mindfulness is about being present, about accepting the world and the moment as we find them. The range of courses and books available suggests a demand for it. On the other side of the coin, despite it being part of philosophical practice in the West since at least Socrates, nobody runs courses in thoughtfulness.

Inspired by popular mindfulness books, I recommend various exercises in thoughtfulness. Hopefully, these will help rekindle the joy of thinking in a busy world full of distractions. The goal is not to foster mere acceptance of the world, but to encourage critical thinking and reflection. The exercises stem from the philosophical tradition of *thought experiments*, which call for a combination of logic, reason and imagination. Different hypothetical scenarios are posited in order to evaluate the nature of knowledge, justice and good deeds. Philosophers do not, of course, conduct real experiments in the empirical world, but their thought experiments help to guide us all towards a more thoughtful, critical and imaginative life. But to get there, we have to think slowly, deeply and for ourselves. Consider, for example, the following classic thought experiment.

Thought experiment 1: Ring of Gyges

Plato's book *The Republic* introduces 'the Ring of Gyges', one of the first thought experiments. It's a good place to start. Plato's brother, Glaucon, formulates it as a kind of challenge to Socrates during a discussion about who is happier, the just or the unjust person. Socrates believes the just person is happier, based on his observation that it is worse to *do* bad than to *suffer* badly. You cannot be happy if you are unjust, because being unjust harms not only your soul, but that of at least one other. At this point, Glaucon introduces the story of the Ring of Gyges, which would undoubtedly have been well known to his listeners. King Gyges had a ring that could make the wearer invisible. (NB: The important aspect of the thought experiment is not how realistic it is, but that it stimulates a discussion about what you would do if you could be invisible – and, indirectly, whether the just or unjust individual is happier.)

Glaucon posits the following:

> Suppose now that there were two such magic rings, and the just put on one of them and the unjust the other; no man can be imagined to be of such an iron nature that he would stand fast in justice. No man would keep his hands off what was not his own when he could safely take what he liked out of the market or go into houses and lie with any one at his pleasure, or kill or release from prison whom he would, and in all respects be like a god among men. Then the actions of the just would be as the actions of the unjust; they would both come at last to the same point. And this we may truly affirm to be a great proof that a man is just, not willingly or because he thinks that justice is any good to him individually, but of necessity, for wherever anyone thinks that he can safely be unjust, there he is unjust.[5]

Introduction

Glaucon imagines a kind of scientific experiment in which both the just and unjust use the ring to make themselves invisible. He argues that the just person will also act in their own interests if a ring conceals their guilt about stealing whatever they want, having sex with whoever they want and killing whoever they want. His analysis is predicated on the idea that only fear of being caught stops us from stealing, raping and killing. Deep down, people are unjust because they believe that what will make them happy isn't justice, but doing whatever they like. And the magic ring allows us to do exactly that. People only act justly when coerced into doing so for fear of reprisal – not because being just in itself makes them happy.

Only much later in *The Republic* does Socrates respond to the challenge and steadfastly defend the idea that just individuals are happier. The essence of his argument is that the problem with the unjust is that they harm themselves *and* others when they do wrong, whereas, by acting in a just manner, the just not only avoid inflicting harm on themselves, but hopefully help others, too. The just are happier because they aren't slaves to the desire for sex, revenge or riches – not even if they happen to be invisible and beyond the reach of justice. The self-control and peace of mind associated with the ability to restrain yourself and just *be* is a prerequisite for a happy life. In fact, *only* the just are happy. As for the concept of justice, Socrates doesn't believe that it reflects what a random majority believes, nor is it the collective shaming of an action that defines its moral quality. To use a modern term, it isn't a 'social construct', but an ideal state that transcends the perspectives of individuals and cultures. In other words, being just and happy is a natural consequence of being a well-rounded person, rather than a matter of coercion.

I hope and believe Socrates is right. Maybe you do, too. Or maybe not? But that's not really the point. Instead, it is that the experiment makes us think, makes us consider eternal philosophical questions: Are good and just actions determined by the conventions of the majority? Are my good deeds ultimately motivated by the desire to be admired by my fellow human beings, or are they driven simply by the inherent value of the good deed? If I could commit all sorts of immoral acts without the risk of being caught, would I have any reason not to?

Questions like these are among the most important we can ask ourselves. And there are no definitive, scientific answers. We need to stop and think about these conundrums and think for ourselves, because they are existential questions about the individual's relationship to others, themselves and their own lives. (I can't just ask others for the answers – not if they are to have fundamental existential meaning for me.) If we want to work towards an answer, we have to allow time for the kind of thoughtful meditation in which the thought experiment invites us to indulge. It doesn't always have to be done alone in a room, in silent contemplation. It can take the form of a conversation, as in the Socratic dialogues, in which Socrates and his interlocutors develop knowledge by stress-testing the views of the others. Thoughtfulness can be a solo or a collective pursuit – as long as our *daimon* is allowed to make itself heard.

*

I hope this ancient thought experiment has whetted your appetite for thoughtfulness. The thinking it requires is of a very different type than that used to work out Kahneman's calculation. Both require slow thinking, but Kahneman's sum has an actual answer, one upon which everybody should ultimately be able to agree. Plato's (or Glaucon's) thought experiment also requires the ability to think rationally, but it is more open. What distinguishes thoughtfulness is the act of rationally thinking about questions to which there is no single answer. As we will see in the next chapter, this is where we can generate meaning in our lives and experiences.

1
What do you think?

Up to this point, it is merely my assertion that modern humans don't think enough – at least in the proper sense of the word – and that it would be good for us, in many ways, to do more of it. If you're with me so far, you probably think there may be something in that assertion. Maybe you know what it's like not having enough time to think deeply and freely and have noted a general lack of critical thinking concerning many of the stories that circulate and go viral on social media.

But even if we perhaps don't think enough, there's no denying that we spend an awful lot of time *talking* about thinking. For example, in books with titles like *Think Before You Speak*, *Think Wild*, *Think Big*, *Think Yourself Healthy*, *Think Yourself Thin*, *Think Your Way to Results*, *Think Your Way to a Good Life*, *Think Like a Woman*, *Think Like a Monk*, *Think Like a Warrior*, *Think Like a Winner*, *Think Your Way Rich*, *Think Again*, *Think Sensitively* and *Think and Get Rich*. Unfortunately, I can't promise that reading this book will make you rich, thin or a winner. It's not about thinking your way to this or that, but more generally about thinking like a human being. In fact, I'm not sure it's even possible to think your way to health, happiness or a good life. But I will argue that we can at least be happy while thinking.

We also spend a lot of time talking about thinking in a different and more specific way. A few years ago, I started to notice that the phrase 'I think' was being used in a new way in Danish – not just as a reference to an actual thought process, as in 'I would prefer not to be interrupted because I am thinking about a difficult problem.' In Danish, we used to think *about* or *over* something, or we would use completely different verbs. We still can, of course, but in recent years it has become increasingly common to drop the prepositions and say things like 'I think we can make the ferry on time', 'I think climate policy will be crucial at the next election' or 'I think Monet was a better painter than Manet'. I first encountered this change in usage when I started to study psychology in the late 1990s.

Strictly speaking, statements like these don't involve thinking – not in the sense encouraged by this book, at any rate. In purely linguistic terms, it is almost certainly an Anglicisation. Previously, the English 'I think' would have been translated differently. But perhaps something else is at play here, too. In both languages, the term is part of a significant shift towards subjective ways of speaking that include expressions like 'I experience', 'I sense' and 'I feel', which are used in everything from sports interviews to university exam assignments. In practice, the modern usage of 'I think' is often synonymous with 'I feel'. We express assertions that are neither thought through nor well founded, but the exact opposite – immediate, non-binding experiences, attitudes and emotions.

I usually avoid acting like the language police, but certain trends in Danish annoy me. I fear that by using expressions like these, our words lack commitment. We use 'I think' or 'I experience' to avoid commitment – emphasising that these are subjective conditions that might change at any moment. They are ephemeral and imply no obligation. Today, you think one thing; tomorrow, probably another. Who cares? There is, of course, room for non-committal communication, but we also need to be able to commit when we make statements. For example, saying 'in my opinion' identifies us with what we say in a more committed manner.

The philosopher of language John Langshaw Austin formulated the theory of speech acts – in brief, that our words function as actions. He argued that, from a functional point of view, all sincere statements are, in effect, promises, as the speaker is bound by their words. If you state sincerely, 'I believe Messi is the world's best football player', you bind yourself. You are obliged to defend this opinion in any ensuing discussion (and must also, of course, be willing to change your mind in the face of superior argumentation). If you just *think* it, in the way the word is now used in Danish, the fact that you assert it doesn't really mean anything. It is just something you 'think', so why bother discussing it? Not that I advocate absolute self-assuredness. My point is that language should retain its binding characteristics precisely so we can learn together by examining each other's assertions about our knowledge and attitudes.

One of the things I want to do with this book is to show that actual thinking is never something we 'just' do, but a realisation of the potential of human nature. Thinking is binding because it requires that we use our reason, which may alter our judgement. This means we are justified when we say things like: 'I have thought it through, weighed up the pros and cons, and am of the considered opinion that the reform of the school system has been a failure.' Language shouldn't be used to reduce thinking to mere guesswork ('I think the reform is bad'). We should continue to insist that thinking involves the studying, testing and justifying of assertions and ideas.

What does the dictionary say?

According to the Danish dictionary, 'think' (*tænke*) has several related meanings. The first is: 'to be aware of your physical experiences; to direct your attention to something particular and, in doing so, acquire greater knowledge or understanding'. The etymology is said to be the Middle Low German *denken*, related to the Old Norse *þekkja*, which means to discover and understand. In other words, in order to grasp the concept of thinking, we need to incorporate other concepts into the process.

'Being aware of your physical experiences' implies that thinking is more than just experiencing something. When watching *The X-Factor* and munching popcorn, you experience the taste of the popcorn and the sound of the songs, but it is only once you become aware that you are experiencing these things that you can be said to be starting to think. There may then be a risk of you wondering whether this is a worthwhile use of your time – and that may not be a pleasant experience. Perhaps the dictionary should specify that thinking is characterised not just by consciousness, but by a sort of *self*-consciousness – because even immediate, thoughtless experience is, of course, also conscious. However, just because an experience is devoid of thought does not necessarily mean that it is devoid of value – indeed, many of the things we value in life prioritise sensory perception over thinking. The point, ultimately, is that it is not until we become aware of something that we can think about it. Consciousness about consciousness is called self-consciousness or self-reflection. That's also why we use prepositions when we talk about thinking – we think *of*, *over* or *about* something. Thinking involves relating to something in a binding way and is closely related to self-consciousness. We don't usually talk about cats, dogs and budgies thinking, even when they stare out the window. They may well be aware of what they are observing, but they're not conscious of being aware of it – and are, therefore, incapable of thinking in the human sense. They lack the capacity for self-reflection and can't think about the fact that they're thinking. A dog may feel a sense of instant gratification if you give it a treat, but it's incapable of thinking about whether it deserved the treat or whether its owner has some kind of ulterior motive, because dogs are incapable of self-reflective thinking.

The other concepts in the dictionary definition are 'attention' and 'knowledge'. Thinking is a process that involves paying attention, which means that we must focus on something in particular rather than everything at the same time. We must immerse ourselves, concentrate on something specific, and shut out everything else. This is far from easy in a world full of distractions, with its constant invitations to scroll, check, click, like and so on. The philosopher and novelist Iris Murdoch described the mastery of thoughtful attention as a form of moral training.[1] She noted, for example, that we often say to children, 'Look, isn't that nice?' or 'Be careful – don't touch that!' as ways of drawing their attention to something specific from a very young age. Learning to pay careful attention is an integral part of learning to think – and according to Murdoch, it is also an integral part of moral training. To learn to think well and deeply, we must learn to dwell on and pay attention to something – on this point at least, mindfulness and thoughtfulness share some common ground. It's good to make developing skills in dwelling on and paying attention to things part of our educational practices – not just for small children (as in Murdoch's example) but in higher education, too. The biologist Erick Greene makes his university students choose a single thing – a tree, a birdhouse, a water hole or whatever – and observe it closely for an entire semester.[2] They then have to write field notes, record what they see and formulate a minimum of ten research questions based on their observations. In his experience, the students' ability to think deeply can be cultivated by patiently paying attention to and dwelling on something in particular. It is an attentive form of thoughtfulness directed outwards at the world.

The final aspect of this definition of thinking is that it improves our understanding or knowledge – the latter in the very broadest sense of the word. Solving Kahneman's sum requires knowledge, of course, but thoughtfulness often leads to thought processes that generate opinions. In such cases, it is not a matter of solving a problem correctly, but of identifying associations, giving our imagination free rein and creating new meaning – including in contexts where we cannot arrive at a definitive answer.

Forms of thinking

Basically, we can distinguish between two forms of thinking: *problem-solving*, in which the assumption is that there is a correct answer to the problem; and *meaning generation*. There is no sharp dividing line between the two, but examples make the difference plain enough. Solving Kahneman's sum is, of course, a matter of solving a problem. It calls for what Kahneman has dubbed system 2 thinking, which is slow and requires mental effort. We need to make calculations and, in that sense, think it *through*.

Thinking as meaning generation is something else. It requires slow thinking as well, but there is rarely a single correct answer – remember Plato's thought experiment in the introduction, or problems you have faced. Most of us are familiar with the experience of *thinking back* to situations that have been formative for the person we have become; social situations which – for better or worse – have shaped our life and personality. This kind of thought process rarely involves solving a problem, although it can incorporate some aspects of that process (if you're wrestling with a difficult moral dilemma, for example). Rather, thinking as meaning generation is related to daydreaming and reverie. Thoughtfulness can also be retroactive (looking back on our lives) or proactive (looking to an as-yet-unknown future). Thinking as meaning generation doesn't need to be about our life, but can be about more general existential or cosmological questions: Is there a God? Is the universe infinite? Is there life after death? What would the ideal society look like? From where does the experience of beauty stem? Do we have a duty to forgive? What is love? There are no single answers to these big existential questions, and the point is not to 'solve the problem' and move on, but to let our minds wander and mull over them. According to the Greek philosophical tradition, which I endorse in this book, it is crucial for a good life that we are able to think in this way.

As well as differentiating between thinking as solving problems and as generating meaning, we can also differentiate between instrumental and intrinsic thinking. This means that thinking can either be a tool (instrumental) in the service of something else, or an end in itself with (intrinsic) value per se. The table below illustrates the two distinctions in a matrix with sharp delineations between them. In reality, the distinctions are not so hard and fast.

Forms of thinking	Problem-solving	Meaning-generating
Instrumental	For example, choosing the right recruit after a job interview	For example, writing an exam essay about your future
Intrinsic	For example, doing a crossword	For example, reflecting freely on the meaning of life

There will often be an overlap between the two distinctions. Thinking as problem-solving usually has instrumental value (which depends on *whether* the problem is solved), while thinking as meaning generation usually has intrinsic value because it is something we do for the activity's own sake. But those are not the only permutations. For example, people who like to do crosswords or sudoku are engaged in a form of problem-solving that appears to have an intrinsic value for them. You can, of course, do that sort of thing to improve your mental fitness – perhaps to be a better stockbroker – but I believe most people do it because they derive some measure of gratification from the immersion and thought activity associated with solving the problem. Similarly, we can think in ways that generate meaning within an instrumental framework, such as when school students are asked to write essays about their future, but only do it to get a good grade, not because they see using their imagination to write about the future as a purpose in itself.

Although we should be wary of ranking the different forms of thinking, it is hard not to notice that children tend to learn – and master – problem-solving before meaning generation. For example, they can be amazing at chess or mathematics – sometimes far better than many adults – but few children write classic novels. The ability needed to do that – to generate meaning in areas where there is no single correct answer – requires a maturity and depth beyond the reach of children. It's not just a matter of pure intelligence, about recognising patterns and finding an answer quickly. It's about life experience and judgement, about cognitive processes that develop much more slowly. Even Plato recommended children learn mathematics before throwing themselves into the type of thinking to which this book invites its readers. Philosophical thoughtfulness calls for a more mature intellect (that was probably what I was subconsciously practising as a child as I lay on the living room floor, letting my mind wander). Even though there is no absolute hierarchy among forms of thinking – because different types are appropriate in different situations – as a general rule we learn one form of thinking before the other and may be good at one of them without necessarily being good at the other.

Thinking in practice

If you were asked to draw something as intangible as 'thoughts' or 'thinking', you would probably draw either a person with a thought bubble containing words or pictures coming out of their head or somebody musing à la Rodin's famous *The Thinker*, who is sitting down, leaning forward, chin on his hand, mulling something over. Or, given the rapid developments in neuroscience in recent decades, a brain scan might spring to mind.[3] All three images represent immediately understandable images for thinking, but they are all a bit too one-dimensional. In fact, that's why none of them has been used as a cover illustration for this book. The cartoon bubble illustrates that thinking can be a form of inner dialogue, but it can also be so much more than that. The same applies, in a sense, to Rodin's sculpture, which portrays thinking as something you do alone, sitting still – which it can be, of course, but doesn't need to be. And the brain scan illustrates the banal truth that the brain is involved in thinking, as well as in every other physical function, but that mustn't mislead us into believing that it's the brain itself that thinks (it's the person), or that thoughts can be reduced to physical/chemical processes in the brain. More on that later. All three images abstract thinking from the practical context in which it usually (if not exclusively) takes place.

One of my favourite thinkers is the philosopher, psychologist, educator and democracy advocate John Dewey (1859–1952). Around a century ago, he developed a pragmatic view of thinking, establishing it as a more down-to-earth and practical activity. I like Dewey because of his sensitive, philosophical nature and his lifelong endeavour to link philosophy to contemporary social issues, both in the United States and around the world. I also like him because he is said to be one of the few educational philosophers to have professed a fondness for children. He appears to have been an inspiring intellectual who managed to combine family life, philosophy and civic duty in a most admirable manner. He thought deeply, abstractly and philosophically, but always with an eye to the world.

Dewey was part of the school of American Pragmatism, which insisted that theories and ideas must be applied in practice and make a difference. It was not a rejection of basic research, the humanities or anything else that doesn't necessarily lead to patents or improve competitiveness. The pragmatists' understanding of practice was particularly broad. For example, Dewey saw thinking as an activity that solves specific problems and leads to more thinking – which some people like to do for its own sake. However, he and the other pragmatists also stress that thinking can be used, first and foremost, to solve problems whenever we find ourselves mired in them, either as individuals or as a collective.

One of Dewey's best-known books was *How We Think* (1910), which outlines the basic pragmatist idea that the ability to think, in the form of self-conscious reflection, is derived from a more direct way of being in the world. In brief, we usually only start to think when we are bogged down in something.[4] In these situations, our habitual actions no longer serve us, and we are forced to stop – and think. For Dewey, thinking and reflection are almost synonymous. Thinking is what you do when you reflect intelligently. He defines reflective thought as an 'active, persistent, and careful consideration of any belief or supposed form of knowledge in the light of the grounds that support it and the further conclusions to which it tends'.[5] Thinking is about testing whether the foundations for your perceptions are solid, and about refining your convictions in the light of new information. By its very nature, this is a reflective process in which you take a step back and evaluate whether what you initially thought still holds. It isn't something people do all the time or just decide to do out of the blue. It is necessitated by a problematic or ambivalent situation in which your habitual activity is getting you nowhere.

Imagine, for example, that you have a problem at work. A colleague proposes a solution, and your first instinct is to reject it. But if you just shoot it down in flames without any thought, you are neglecting to consider their view 'in the light of the grounds that support it'. The idea might actually be excellent, and your antipathy towards it a manifestation of jealousy at the colleague being promoted because they generate so many good ideas – maybe more than you do. Alternatively, the idea might well be problematic –

irrespective of whether you are jealous – but separating the two elements (the actual proposal and the person putting it forward) requires you to stop and think again. Thinking almost always requires that you slow down before making a decision and taking action.

Thinking always begins with what Dewey called 'a forked-road situation'. He subdivides the reflective thinking process into five steps: (1) identify the problem; (2) investigate/analyse the problem; (3) generate several possible solutions; (4) evaluate the options and choose the best solution or combination of solutions; and (5) test and deploy the solution. It is essential to be aware that thinking encompasses the whole of this process, not just elements of it. For example, some modern cognitive psychologists understand thinking as the fourth step, when we use reason and attempt to formulate algorithms or rules for the process. Dewey would insist that it's meaningless to take one step in isolation from the others. He also argued that it's impossible to formulate general rules or principles for reflective thinking. In his opinion, thinking is linked to experience in a specific area, and so can't exist independently of the content of the thoughts. Thinking isn't a pure process or form we can understand without content or material, just as digestion can't be understood in isolation from food intake. We always think *of* or *about*. Thinking is determined by content. This means we're not necessarily good at thinking scientifically just because we're good at thinking narratively and writing literature – or vice versa. We can't be good at thinking as such, but we can be good at thinking *about* certain questions, *in* certain ways, *in* certain situations, etc. Again, the preposition is really important.

Even if thinking is content-specific, it doesn't mean that all forms of thinking are adaptable for use in a specific area. For example, Dewey was well aware that thinking can also be about solving second-degree equations or using formal logic to formulate an argument. He calls this abstract thinking and differentiates it from the concrete form – which is a means to an end other than just thinking. For example, when we think about how to get from A to B, our thinking is valid if we make it from A to B in an appropriate manner. The intention behind abstract thinking, on the other hand, is not to achieve an external goal, but that it will lead to more thinking. In this instance, the goal is something inherent in the means – in using the means in a better way. An example of this might be solving equations for no other reason than to solve equations. This is Dewey's version of what I previously called intrinsic thinking. According to Dewey, this form of thinking for thinking's sake fulfils an important function in our life: 'Interest in knowledge for the sake of knowledge, in thinking for the sake of the free play of thought, is necessary to the *emancipation* of practical life – to making it rich and progressive.'[6] Thinking for its own sake may not remove us from all the problems of practical life, but we acquire 'a certain magnanimity and richness of imagination in our method of observation', which can be helpful when we seek to improve our life. If we can't appreciate thinking for its own sake, we will lack generosity of spirit and imagination. This is an important argument in favour of basic research: even if we can't directly translate basic research into better treatments, patents or useful products, just becoming wiser can be valuable per se as it expands our horizons and improves the intellect.

Intrinsic thinking is imaginative and generous of spirit precisely because it lifts us above day-to-day chores and ultimately endows our lives with meaning. The reason that we reflect at all, according to Dewey, is that a certain situation reveals the absence of meaning, i.e. it is unclear how a specific event we encounter should be understood in relation to the mass of events that makes up our life. For example, if we see something incomprehensible – say, a person waving their arms about on the other side of the road – then we have to think in order to place the immediately incomprehensible into a meaningful context. It might be that from our vantage point we can't see a wasp buzzing around the person's head. That would explain the movements – make them meaningful – and we can use this explanation until we know more or better. This way of thinking is called *abduction*, in which we accept the best explanation (as opposed to *induction*, where we work from the specific to the general; and *deduction*, where we move from the general to the specific). Abduction consists of, firstly, generating meaning in practice through thinking; secondly, testing this meaning in real life now and in the future; and thirdly, being willing to revise what we thought in the light of new knowledge or encountering better reasons to believe something else. Abduction, as a basic way of thinking, is pragmatism's major contribution to philosophy.

One big problem with human thinking is that it's difficult to break with our convictions, even when there is good reason to do so. For example, we tend to seek out and choose the information that supports what we believe instead of considering points that run *counter* to our beliefs. This is called *confirmation bias*. Thinking well and thinking for yourself must also include thinking *self-critically*. We need to be aware of the tendency towards confirmation bias, to which we all are susceptible to some extent or another. Dewey argues that reflective and self-critical thinking is a habit we can learn, just like all kinds of other habits. He claims that the primary goal of education and upbringing is to cultivate habits that encourage thinking. I will return to this in a later chapter. However, this doesn't mean that schools and higher education institutions should introduce subjects or modules that deal explicitly with thinking. There is plenty of evidence (including in Dewey's writings) to suggest that thinking is best cultivated by the existing disciplines, so that it is linked to specific content. We can learn to think better in a history class by wondering how history unfolded the way it did. In other subjects, we might think mathematically, in a literary way, aesthetically or practically. Thinking isn't a subject in its own right because ultimately all disciplines involve it. As the psychologist Barry Schwartz put it: any teacher will, more than anything else, want their students to learn to think. And yet, we rarely think about what we mean by thinking.[7]

We now leave Dewey with the insight that thinking, as a rule, begins with a problem we need to address, on which we must reflect and think in order to move forward. But a more relaxed form of thinking also comes to us in situations where we are not necessarily bogged down. We will return to this in Chapter 2 when discussing how Martin Heidegger, in particular, challenges the lack of thinking in the modern age. To sum up, thinking can be both an active part of our life, as stressed by Dewey, and part of a life in which we sit back and dwell on matters, as illustrated by Heidegger.

Thought experiment 2: The trolley problems

In the previous chapter, I presented an ancient thought experiment from Plato. This time, the example is more recent. In 1967, the philosopher Philippa Foot wrote about what has become known as 'the trolley problem'.[8] In this experiment, a trolley bus (a kind of tram) is out of control, hurtling towards five oblivious people walking along the track. Imagine you're watching the catastrophe about to unfold, but you can pull a lever, switch the trolley to another track and save the five people's lives. However, the trolley would instead plough into a single innocent person walking on the other track. So, the question is: should you sacrifice one person to save five others? Most people say yes, based on an intuitive utilitarianism, according to which you should seek the best possible outcome for the maximum number of people. However, if you believe that an action has independent value, it becomes more complicated – because in pulling that lever, you actively decide to kill someone. Is there a difference between letting something happen without intervening (even though you could) and active intervention? Indeed, is *not* acting actually an action in itself? These are some of the issues the experiment encourages us to consider.

Another philosopher, Judith Jarvis Thomson, later added an extra twist (it was Thomson who dubbed it the trolley problem).[9] She asks you to imagine you're standing on a bridge above the tracks and the only way to stop the runaway trolley bus is to throw an obese person onto the tracks (you're too much of a lightweight to stop it with your own bulk). Structurally, it's the same situation with the same mathematical logic: save five by sacrificing one. However, experience shows that fewer people will say yes to killing an innocent person if it involves shoving the person concerned off the bridge and onto the tracks – even if it does save five lives. What we see here is that our thoughts about what is right in the situation are not independent of our emotional response to the prospect of grabbing hold of somebody and throwing them off a bridge. That seems even more unacceptable than pulling a lever, even though we know that failing to take this action will have the same fatal consequences. The question is whether our emotions help us to see the situation more clearly – so we understand it is not just a mathematical problem of saving as many as possible but also a question of the moral responsibility implied by our intervention. Or is it that our emotions play tricks on us, rendering us incapable of objective thought? I tend to go with the first explanation. Mull it over and see what you think. I will return to the role emotions play in our thinking in the final chapter of the book.

In a third variant of the experiment (again by Thomson), you are a doctor who could save five people in an intensive care ward, each of whom needs a vital organ transplant. To do so, you need to drug and kill one innocent person. Perhaps the postie at the remote hospital during a snowstorm early one winter morning? You could harvest their organs and transplant them into the five dying patients. In this case, I would guess that more or less everybody would think it's wrong in principle to kill the innocent person to save the other five. Again, the maths is the same as the original situation, but most of us now have little trouble concluding that we shouldn't make an innocent person an instrument in this way – even in the service of a good cause such as saving other people's lives. But why do so many (even you?) tend to think that it is okay in the original version of the trolley problem? Perhaps the proximity to the innocent person means something. Or maybe the degree of active intervention – shoving or lethal injection – is relevant. Think about it. Ask your friends and family what they think. The question offers a fascinating insight into people and their ethical outlook. Should you sacrifice one to save the many? Do we even have a duty to do so?

2

Why has it become difficult to think?

Something about the very idea of the thoughtful life seems out of step with the times. Sociologists have long described and analysed the phenomenon of social acceleration observable in just about anything quantifiable.[1] We sleep less and change jobs, homes and partners more often. We use technology in the home and at work – everything from email to dishwashers – to enhance efficiency, and yet it still seems to be more of a time thief than a time saver. Despite (or perhaps because of) the ease of sending emails, US studies show that office workers spend more than five hours a day dealing with them.[2] By its very nature, sending old-fashioned post requires relatively careful thought – composing the letter, maybe even writing it by hand, buying a stamp and putting it in a post box. It's a far cry from dashing off an email about whatever is on our minds, which costs nothing and arrives almost instantly. Communication technology has had a huge impact on how easy or difficult it is to think in day-to-day life, including at work. The speed at which we consume culture has also intensified. YouTube, iTunes and Netflix all let you speed up videos, podcasts and movies, so you can fit in more in less time. Some eBook readers also have features to optimise reading speed. Do we really have enough time to think about everything we consume?

All this is well known and has attracted a great deal of criticism, but not enough light has been shone on the consequences for thoughtfulness. Thinking well, profoundly and critically requires time for reflection and afterthought. As Dewey noted, we usually start to think when things don't work, when we harbour doubts about something unclear or complicated. Ergo, the more technology simplifies things and improves efficiency, the more difficult it is to think because thinking depends on the ability not to react in a knee-jerk manner, to postpone decisions, consult other people, listen to their experiences and arguments and consider the matter properly. Although new technology is often developed with the best of intentions – to make life easier and perhaps even free up time for a thoughtful life – the reality is often the opposite. We enter into a spiral of ever-increasing speed, which also, of course, triggers a backlash in the form of self-help books about the slow life, meditation and mindfulness. Paradoxically, some of these solutions present themselves as quick fixes (one-week courses, weekend retreats and seven-step guides to a better life, etc.), despite the fact that the original premise is that everything is moving far too fast.

In this situation, it's important to point out that the thoughtful life is a slow fix. You can't really programme yourself to live a thoughtful life by stopping to think for ten minutes every night before bed. Ultimately, a more thoughtful life also calls for schools, institutions and workplaces that allow time and space for unhurried afterthought and critical analysis. The problem is that as progress accelerates, people have to enhance their skills just as quickly to keep up, whereas the benefits of thoughtfulness are anything but immediate, which makes it seem like a waste of time. Nevertheless, it is this apparent lack of purpose we need most.

Philosophical thought emerged in ancient Greece as precisely that – a form of thinking deemed to have no purpose, which is why it was often considered dangerous. Socrates was sentenced to death for 'corrupting the youth' with useless questions such as: What is beauty? What is love? Can virtue be learned? Socrates died for philosophy, much as Jesus did for faith. The form of thoughtfulness practised by Socrates (at least in some of Plato's dialogues) entailed asking questions and examining assertions without necessarily arriving at answers. According to Plato, philosophy originates from wonder, which ought, of course, to be relatively harmless. But that isn't necessarily the case. What if people wonder why wealth is unequally distributed, why tyrants apparently often live happy lives, or about how to create a fairer society? The powers that were in ancient Greece had no time for that sort of wondering – and the powers that be today still don't. Socrates' philosophical approach doesn't provide unambiguous answers but it does insist on not taking anything for granted. Everything can be studied and criticised, and not just on the basis of hunches and gut feelings, but by deploying clear-headed critical thinking and reasoned arguments.

The contemporary philosopher Simon Critchley adds that philosophy originates not only from wonder but also from disappointment[3] – including disappointment that no omnipotent interventionist God is on hand to guarantee all is well in the world, and disappointment at the lack of fairness in society. Those who believe in an all-merciful God may have no use for philosophy, but Critchley says that unless you're convinced faith can cover everything, you need philosophy, too. Many in ancient Greece felt this need, and various schools of philosophy flourished, each of which had its own way of engaging in a thoughtful life. One of the more curious examples was Diogenes, who belonged to the Cynical School, albeit he wasn't a cynic in the modern sense of the word. The term actually referred to the fact that he lived a bit like a dog (*kyon* in Greek). He had little regard for public morality, and legend has it he lived in a barrel. Legend also has it that the most powerful man in the ancient world, Alexander the Great, sought him out one day to reward the unique philosopher for his wisdom, but all Diogenes wanted was for Alexander to move slightly to the side because he was blocking the sun. On the one hand, the story is perfectly innocent, about someone who has recognised what is truly valuable in life. On the other, it's potentially subversive because anyone with the courage to say no to the rulers' sticks and (in this case) carrots, lives their life according to higher purposes than power, status and prestige. That was precisely how Diogenes lived, as did several other philosophers in his day, and that made them dangerous. Thoughtfulness is potentially dangerous because it may lead people to question what otherwise appears to be self-evident. Philosophical afterthought often takes the form of a kind of denaturalisation, in which we stop taking things for granted, wonder why they are the way they are, and imagine how they could be different. This is also the classic structure of a thought experiment. In an age of social acceleration, when what we do is expected to be useful, thoughtfulness seems more necessary than ever. It acts like a tiny stone in our shoe, making us stop, sit down and look closely at what is bothering us.

An age without thought

In the introduction, I mentioned Martin Heidegger's cultural criticism and how he highlighted the lack of thinking in his day. Heidegger articulated his critique after the Second World War, during which his own support for Nazism testified to a catastrophic lack of thinking. Historians and philosophers have long debated whether Heidegger's Nazism was a personal moral shortcoming or an inherent part of his philosophy. If the latter is the case, we can't now use his work at all. What we do know for sure is that he joined the Nazi Party when he was appointed Rector of the University of Freiburg in 1933 and stopped attending party meetings when he resigned from the post a year later. Shamefully, however, he remained an actual member until the end of the war. Nevertheless, I am one of those who think that it is still worthwhile reading Heidegger, and that his philosophy is not in itself contaminated by Nazism in a fundamentally damaging way.

Why has it become difficult to think? 33

Heidegger is an important thinker for many reasons. In the context of this book, his analysis of the conditions faced by thinking in a culture dominated by technology and instrumentalism is fascinating. In *What is Called Thinking?*, which consists of lectures from the early 1950s, Heidegger writes, as previously quoted, "what is most thought-provoking in our thought-provoking time is that we are still not thinking'.[4] According to him, modern humans are deeply concerned with evidence, utility and utility value, yet lack the ability to think. Heidegger focuses on this development in particular in an essay written in the early 1950s on the question of technology.[5] He first rejects a simple instrumental understanding of technology, which asserts that we should understand it as a means of realising certain human intentions. It is a very familiar idea: we can use a knife to cut bread for the poor, or we can use it to cut someone's throat. Technology is inherently value-neutral. Only through the intentions and application of humans does it become good or evil. However, according to Heidegger, that is a superficial understanding, given that technology has to do with the way humankind is in the world. Technology is one way in which the world reveals itself. For Heidegger, technology 'is therefore no mere means. Technology is a way of revealing.'[6]

In other words, technology, like religion or aesthetics, is essentially a means of understanding the world around us. Indeed, the fact that we use technology in this way may even be the defining characteristic of modern life. Technology reveals the world in a way in which things are identified as resources (*Bestand* in German). Or, as Heidegger explains in his characteristically complicated manner: 'Everywhere everything is ordered to stand by, to be immediately on hand, indeed, to stand there just so that it may be on call for a further ordering. Whatever is ordered about in this way has its own standing. We call it the standing-reserve [Bestand].'[7] This part of Heidegger is not easy to translate, but *Bestand* has been rendered as 'standing reserve' – something we can mobilise and use when needed. Technology makes the world a reservoir of resources that exist for the sake of humankind. Heidegger believes that this approach to the world may not be wrong per se but tends to marginalise other necessary perspectives.

Further examples from Heidegger's analysis might aid understanding. Technology reveals that forests are timber, which can be used by humans in construction projects. This makes forests 'standing reserves' for human needs – which is all well and good, of course, provided we bear in mind other perspectives, such as the value of the biodiversity in the forest, which may clash with human intentions. Wind is revealed to be energy we can generate in turbines. Humans are revealed as production units we can optimise to work efficiently. According to Heidegger, there is nothing inherently wrong with any of that, but it may well make us forget the other ways in which we can relate to the world. Modernity sees pretty much everything as a resource. Heidegger was writing about this in the early 1950s, but he sounds remarkably prophetic when he trains his analytical eye on humanity, asking: 'does not man himself belong even more originally than nature within the standing-reserve? The current talk about human resources, about the supply of patients for a clinic, gives evidence of this.'[8]

In the decades since Heidegger wrote this, we have witnessed the emergence of human resource management and self-optimisation practices, not just in workplaces, but more or less everywhere in modern states – often conceptualised under the heading 'the competition state' – including in their education systems. Perhaps it has become even more challenging to think about people and their activities in terms other than utility value, development and optimisation. Even knowledge, art and literature are increasingly instrumentalised and evaluated according to their contribution to GDP, public health, happiness or other external goals.[9] Of course, it is not only Heidegger and his intellectual heirs who have noticed and analysed these relationships. There is also a long Marxist tradition of analysing instrumentalisation as part and parcel of capitalism's built-in tendency towards growth and optimisation. Marxists say that selling your labour as a commodity is alienating and turns people and their activities into commodities. Marx saw technology – especially new industrial machines – as the means of production. He believed that while the craftsman used tools, the factory worker was reduced to being a tool used by the machine.[10] Marx thought the problem was linked to class conflict and capitalism. Heidegger believed it was a much older problem associated with Western thinking in general. He at least offers some hope that we can still think in ways other than the instrumental – through art, for example – while Marx sees social revolution as a prerequisite for a different way of thinking. Such a revolution has yet to materialise, and so in the meantime Heidegger is the main source of my critique of our failure to think about thinking.

For Heidegger, the question of technology doesn't reflect a romantic longing for a pre-civilised world in the spirit of the Swiss-French Enlightenment philosopher Jean-Jacques Rousseau (famous for his often-misunderstood slogan 'Back to Nature!'). Nor does he seek to deny its benefits. He wants to know how we have come to take for granted this impoverished way of relating to the world, from which thinking is disappearing. He describes how 'dwelling' or being in the world (*wohnen* in German) has been forgotten. This is problematic because the technological perspective limits our understanding. To 'inhabit', *wohnen* or dwell (as Heidegger dramatically put it, 'man dwells on this earth')[11] is about being situated somewhere, about relating to our existence and finiteness – it is about *caring*. Things are meaningful to us precisely because we live in a specific place. In this sense, dwelling is a contemplative state of being, one based on thoughtfulness, which makes it possible for the world to appear non-instrumental. We can only think, in the real sense of the word, when we are able to dwell.

To illuminate Heidegger's somewhat obscure arguments, the American philosopher and interpreter of Heidegger, Hubert Dreyfus, uses the everyday example of an ordinary cup.[12] In Dreyfus's day in the West (and increasingly, in most of the world today), it was normal to use mass-produced, disposable Styrofoam cups to keep drinks at a constant temperature. The cup is functional and purely instrumental. By contrast, a Japanese teacup is charged with cultural significance, and plays a role in various rituals handed down from generation to generation. The Japanese teacup is not just a tool that makes it possible to consume a resource. It not only offers an instrumental relationship to the world but reveals a complete cultural understanding of what it means to be an object of this kind (delicate, beautiful, traditional) and how this meshes with the understanding of what it means to be human (patient, content, gentle, social) in Japan. The teacup positions the human as a thoughtful, dwelling being whose relationships to the world are at least partly non-instrumental. The mass-produced Styrofoam cup, on the other hand, positions the human being as efficient and controlling in a world of resources that have to be exploited as well as possible. The Styrofoam cup is produced in factories; the teacup by master craftspeople.

At the risk of oversimplification, we might say that (among other things) dwelling-based thinking is about understanding an object's (in this case, a teacup's) many meanings and relationships, whereas the lack of actual thinking involved in the use of technology only teaches us about utility value. From this perspective, thinking is about being able to see the trees as trees in a forest. It's a matter of seeing the world independently of our instrumental relationships with it. Conversely, opportunism consists of seeing the trees as mere timber.

But there's no reason to resort to conspiracy theories. No shadowy cabal is discouraging us from thinking and forcing us to relate instrumentally to the world. Failure to think is a clear and long-term historical trend. Fortunately, we now have a better-educated population with increasingly easy access to vast amounts of information, not least through the internet. And yet, paradoxically, it's precisely this technology that is making thinking more difficult. At least, that is, if Heidegger is right that a technological understanding of the world invites instrumentalism and opportunism by prioritising accessibility, speed and usefulness over attention, dwelling and thoughtfulness. I return to this in subsequent chapters, in an attempt to counter this tendency. In Chapter 3, I describe the joys of rediscovering non-instrumental thinking, and in Chapter 4, I offer a perspective on how thinking is related to the concept defined in the introduction as formation.

Virtues of thinking

First, I want to explore some of the characteristics of thoughtfulness. Later, I will focus on these in greater depth by referring to the continental European tradition in philosophy that runs from Aristotle to Hannah Arendt and Hans-Georg Gadamer and stresses the existential dimensions of thinking. But it is also worth looking at the tradition of clear thinking and critical thought in English-language philosophy. In this tradition, 'virtue epistemology' is the modern equivalent of Aristotle's ideas. Linda Zagzebski is one prominent advocate of this approach. In *Virtues of the Mind*,[13] she shifts the focus from traditional epistemological questions, which are solely preoccupied with the nature of people's beliefs ('what can I know?'), to questions regarding the nature of the conscious human being ('how must I *be* in order to know?').

Virtue epistemology can also address the question of whether we have a duty to have the correct beliefs. That may sound like a strange question: Do we have a duty to think well, in the same way we do to act well? In other words, can we only talk about (ethical) duties in terms of our *actions*, or can we also discuss duties via the lens of our (epistemic) *beliefs*? *Episteme* means true knowledge, so it's a crucial question whether we have a duty to seek true knowledge or whether our only duty is to act well. Often, the two questions are interconnected since the virtuous act is often contingent on true knowledge.

Virtue epistemology seeks to blur the sharp distinctions between the good and the true and between ethics and epistemology, which is also in keeping with the Aristotelian and ancient traditions. Aristotle developed an understanding of humankind based on the concept of virtue.[14] The central idea is that humans – like everything else in the universe – must be understood in relation to their purpose. Aristotle's teachings about humankind are in effect a virtue ethics, in that the virtues themselves are the attributes that allow beings to realise their inherent purpose. According to Aristotle, humans are the only creatures endowed with both theoretical and practical reason, which is why we have the ability to think scientifically and philosophically about the world. This is the field of theoretical reason, but also encompasses practical reason, which implies an ability to act in a morally responsible manner. Only humans – not animals – are held morally responsible for their deeds. Similarly, we think only humans seek out knowledge of the universe for the sole reason that learning has intrinsic value. According to Aristotle, to do these things is to do something that is its own purpose. The ethically good act has value not only because it may bring the person honour or fame, but because doing good has value in and of itself. The value of learning about planets and solar systems lies not in how it contributes to the nation's competitiveness or GDP – rather, acquiring such knowledge has value per se. The attributes a person needs in order to realise their own human nature and to live a thriving, full life (which the Greeks called *eudaimonia*) are the virtues. Humankind and its virtues must be nurtured if we are to realise our purpose and become, in the truest sense, human beings. This process of cultivation takes place in the *polis*, the Greek city state, which makes all human formation political by nature.

A virtue is, therefore, what enables something to realise its inner purpose, be it a knife, the virtue of which is to cut well (which is clearly the characteristic that makes a good knife good), or a human being, the virtues of which are multifaceted, but undeniably involve reason. As a consequence, in order to understand what a human being is, we must understand the virtues that enable us to be good people (just as a knife can only be understood if we know what a knife does – cuts well – when it does what it is meant to). As such, the idea of a *good* person is, in some ways, more fundamental than just our idea of a human being. In other words, we are judged on our potential to be prime examples of our species. According to virtue thinking, we must know what we *could* become in order to find out what we already *are* – and what we could ultimately become is a *thinking* being.

According to this Greek way of thinking, becoming a human being means realising our potential. The potential in question isn't about becoming 'the best version of ourself', as unique individuals, which in the modern era we cultivate under the guise of self-development. No, it's about becoming a (better) human being. Aristotle's philosophy unfolds here in a field of tension between the active life – in which the focus is on noble, courageous actions and political participation, as activities that have intrinsic value – and the thoughtful or contemplative life, in which immersion in existential, ethical and cosmological questions is considered an end in itself. For example, as humans we can derive deep joy from looking at the stars and contemplating our minuteness in the vastness of the universe. Aristotle sees this as an activity that contributes to our ability to thrive precisely because it is not instrumentally useful. Seen through an Aristotelian lens, humans are the only beings capable of thinking for no purpose other than to think. The cultivation of that ability is, therefore, a crucial component of the concept of formation, as we will see in a later chapter.

For Aristotle, the virtues are ideally determined between two extreme poles, as illustrated by the phrase 'virtue lies in the middle'. Courage, for example, is an ethical virtue – something that, according to Aristotle, is necessary to live a full, thriving human life. The brave person is one who finds a balance between cowardice on the one hand and foolhardiness on the other. Being brave is not the same as being careless or completely free of anxiety and worries. It's about daring to do the right thing, even when afraid. The coward doesn't dare to do anything, while the foolhardy person plunges headlong into all sorts of rash actions. Both are equally wrong-headed. The virtue – and hence the good person – is found in the middle, between these outer poles. This means that moderation, understood as the ability to balance sensibly between extremes, itself becomes a key virtue. The good person knows, for example, that generosity is good, certainly better than stinginess, but that immoderately giving everything away to the extent you can't feed yourself and your children is not good. The moderate person strikes a balance between meanness and boundless generosity, between cowardice and recklessness, between having no friends and being 'friends' with everyone, and so on.

Discussions of Aristotle's philosophy frequently stress these moral characteristics, but in the context of this book the interesting point is that the attributes associated with good thinking are also essential for the good life. According to Aristotle, if you're not able to think well, there is, in some sense, something wrong with you, for which you could be held responsible. Just as we have a moral duty to act well, we also have a moral duty to think well. This is fundamental to a good and full human existence. If you doubt this, consider people who hold strange beliefs (conspiracy theorists and flat-Earthers, for example). Even when such beliefs are totally innocuous, many of us will probably feel that whoever holds them isn't just wrong but has some kind of duty to wise up. We believe (or at least I do) that a person's life is better, in the sense of fuller, if they stick roughly to the facts – even when the facts are relatively inconsequential to our actions (it makes little practical difference whether you think the Earth is flat or not). All of us have a certain number of wrong beliefs, but if the virtues of thinking are sufficiently developed, we should be interested in forming truer thoughts and beliefs. We do this not just to turn ourselves into more valuable fodder for the labour market, but because we recognise that good thinking has value per se – even if we don't need to take tests or sit exams in it. Some of the relevant virtues in terms of thinking are:

- Objectivity: The ability to transcend your subjective biases
- Curiosity: The desire to be surprised in order to learn
- Doubt: The willingness to consider the validity of your own perspective
- Thoroughness: The striving to continue to verify your beliefs

We might also add honesty, humility, ingenuity, and so much more to this list. All of these values ought to be part of the scientific ethos, but essentially function as more general aspirations. What they have in common is that they demonstrate that discussions of knowledge and science are not about who is right, persuading others to agree with us, or finding definitive truths. Instead, they are about participating in the production of the most certain and reliable knowledge possible. These virtues are also about countering confirmation bias – as mentioned earlier, the tendency to seek out information that reaffirms views we already hold. This tendency is, unfortunately, particularly marked in an era of access to all kinds of digital and social media, which feed us more of what we already believe. A key point is that the virtues of thinking, as well as the ethical virtues, are characteristics that must be cultivated and acquired collectively, along with others. As the developmental scientist Barbara Rogoff has shown, thinking, like other human abilities, is acquired through a kind of apprenticeship.[15] Just as we learn to talk by conversing with others, we learn to think along with others. Thinking is something that takes place first as a collective human activity. Only later does the individual engage in it alone. Socrates is only able to consult his *daimon* in solitary majesty because he brought it to life through dialogue with his parents and teachers. We learn to relate thoughtfully to our own lives through others relating thoughtfully to us. I will return to this point towards the end of the book.

The humanities as meaningful thinking

The humanities have long provided an institutional framework for thoughtfulness in the West. Historically, these subjects have been highly significant in cultivating the virtues of thinking. In a resolute defence of humanities disciplines such as philosophy, history, language and literature, the philosopher Martha Nussbaum writes that they offer insights that are of intrinsic value in our lives.[16] Her argument is that it is from the humanities in particular that we derive our understanding of what it means to be citizens in a democracy, which she considers a purpose in itself. Being a citizen in a democracy should not just be quantified by external yardsticks (GDP or competitiveness, for example) but understood as something that has its own innate value for people who want to live freely together while acknowledging that this comes with duties. Being a well-rounded person who understands their fellow human beings, who knows about their native language and the history of their nation, as well as other languages and cultures, is not just a means to an end, but is in itself the realisation of a democratic life with intrinsic value. The title of Nussbaum's book, *Not for Profit*, alludes to her belief that the forms of knowledge and skill cultivated and imparted by the humanities mustn't (just) be assessed on whether the nation is growing richer economically, but (also and especially) on whether they enable citizens to live thriving democratic lives with one another.

As a philosopher, one of Nussbaum's projects concerned democratic awareness in India. It is her contention that, in recent years, countries all over the world have been neglecting study programmes that keep the flag of democracy flying. This is also the case in Denmark, where the humanities have been subject to heavy spending cuts for many years. Sometimes they are accused of having too little relevance to society (the charge being that humanities subjects equip graduates only for unemployment while enabling researchers to sit in ivory towers). And yet, sometimes, their influence on society is deemed excessive (see the discussion about political activism among academics in the humanities raised by Danish politicians such as Morten Messerschmidt and Henrik Dahl, who are sceptical about the influence of gender and minority studies in particular). But why this emphasis on the humanities? Would it not be just as legitimate to say that the natural and health sciences offer knowledge of benefit to democracies? And what about the technical and engineering sciences? Indeed, these disciplines provide plenty of relevant knowledge, and no modern democracy can do without them. It is extremely relevant to develop knowledge about vaccines, cancer treatments, soil acidification and microchips – not only because this allows us to file patents and improve competitiveness, but also because the knowledge acquired has value just by dint of us learning about the world. However, the humanities have an additional component that is less obvious in other disciplines: they are about meaning. The natural sciences uncover causal processes in nature (e.g. what is the relationship between CO_2 emissions and global warming?), whereas the humanities uncover and interpret links between meaning (e.g. what characterises the auto-fictional wave in modern literature?).

It is precisely because the humanities relate to meaning rather than causes that they help nurture a form of thinking that generates meaning. Philosophical reflections – as illustrated in the thought experiments in this book, for example – call for imagination and judgement. They can't be 'solved' by knowing about causal relationships in nature. Understanding literature, cultural history, language and other peoples both presupposes and cultivates imagination and judgement, because all of these areas revolve around meaning. It is still relevant to study and discuss Greek philosophy, Cervantes' writings, Shakespeare's dramas and Inger Christensen's poems, because meaning does not become obsolete in the same way as knowledge of causal relationships. New artistic idioms and genres emerge all the time, but they don't consign previous genres and works to the dustbin of history. No one can meaningfully say that Yahya Hassan's recent poems have replaced those of Inger Christensen in the Danish literary canon. In the natural sciences, the opposite is the case. We no longer study Aristotle's physics precisely because it *is* obsolete. Indeed, we only ever study scientific theories that have falsified older ones. Although the meaning generated by the humanities is in a constant state of flux, older texts and cultural idioms are often fruitful parts of new contexts of meaning because, in principle, it is via the humanistic legacy as a whole that we are connected to our history. Our language, our religion, our traditions, our ethical values, our habits, our institutions, our symbols, etc., collectively provide a basis on which to understand and interpret ourselves. Without that, we would not be able to function as a democratic society, because we would have no idea how we came to be the way we are. We would not – and could not – know what is important. In short, the world would be meaningless, and we would be unable to think meaningfully.

Nussbaum concludes that it is the humanities, more than anything else, that teach us to think critically, transcend local boundaries and put ourselves in other people's shoes. And that has never been more important. Acquiring these abilities trains us in democracy because in order to function a democracy requires citizens who are active, critical and able to resist external pressures. In short, good democracy presupposes good thinking. Inherent in democracy is an ideal of formation that is deeply interwoven with the ability to think, in the sense of generating meaning. The thought experiment below – a kind of political fantasy – requires precisely that ability.

Thought experiment 3: Behind the veil of ignorance

John Rawls was one of the most influential political philosophers of the twentieth century. He is best known for his theory of justice, which was published in a book of the same name in the early 1970s.[17] In it, he defended a view of social justice as fairness, but what most people remember from the book is the famous thought experiment on the veil of ignorance.

The idea is to imagine living in a future society, but with no knowledge of your place in it or how it is organised. In other words, you live behind a veil of ignorance that obscures the circumstances of your life. You have no idea whether you're male or female, rich or poor, black or white, homosexual or heterosexual, or something completely different. Imagine the experiment as a lottery, in which you draw a number that determines your position in society. The idea is to think about what we really understand by a just society. After all, if we don't know what our place will be in the social hierarchy, we are free to think in ways not influenced by privilege and resources – or a lack of them. If impartial reason alone were used to inform the creation of a just society, what would it look like? Would it be relatively equal or unequal, have widespread or little redistribution of wealth, an emphasis on individual freedom or collective cohesion? Just ponder these ideas for a moment.

My point in mentioning Rawls' thought experiment is not to convey the conclusions he draws from it himself. Rather, it's that it would probably promote critical thinking about any given society if, once in a while, we were to take a step back and consider whether it could be better and fairer. If you're curious as to how Rawls himself approaches the thought experiment, it goes something like this: He thinks it would be rational to create a society on the basis of a principle of freedom – in other words, the principle that says every citizen has basic freedoms. Thankfully, this is relatively uncontroversial in my part of the world. But he also believes it would be rational for society to be relatively equal, and for inequalities to be minimised to benefit the most disadvantaged. In short, once we lift the veil of ignorance and see the basic structure of society – its 'original position' – we would choose to create one in which the most disadvantaged enjoy the best possible conditions. After all, if social roles are handed out at random, everyone is at risk of being the least privileged. However, this doesn't mean that the ideal and most just society is perfectly equal. It's entirely conceivable that a society that supports freedom of initiative and leads to inequality might make the poor more prosperous than redistribution would have done.

All in all, we can conclude that Rawls himself thought that the most just society is one that maintains a balance between equality and freedom. In other words, it is a place where the weakest have the best possible conditions. As the famous Danish singer Kim Larsen reportedly said: 'I can't understand what government is for if it's not to protect the weak. The strong will be fine.' I think Rawls would agree. I also think Denmark is one of the countries that come closest to striking that balance. But before we Danes pat ourselves on the back too much, it is worth noting the criticisms that have been levelled at Rawls' experiment. His critics insist that there is something artificial about this exercise – after all, you can't just abstract a society out of time, place and history, and design everything from scratch. A society is what it is precisely because of its historical evolution. Perhaps you have to share Rawls' worldview to see the sense in a thought experiment that reduces society to a blank slate.

I understand that criticism, and the experiment does have a utopian aspect, but I would argue that pondering such political problems and debates stimulates our critical faculties. The veil remains a landmark thought experiment and has played a major role in one of the most important debates within political philosophy in recent decades – between communitarianism (in which the self is embedded in communities) and liberalism (which emphasises the rights of the free individual).

Whichever side you take in this debate, it's probably worth spending some time looking behind the veil of ignorance.

How to think critically

If it's correct that an accelerating and opportunistic world makes it harder to think, then little wonder so many books devoted to resurrecting the ability to think critically have been published of late. The sociologist Rasmus Willig has spent years analysing how the conditions for criticism have changed.[18] The outward-looking social criticism of previous decades – the 1970s, for example – is gradually being supplanted by an introspective self-criticism. We are told not to make ourselves 'victims' of external circumstances by being critical of them, but to 'start with the self', 'think positively' and 'look to the future'. It is often the critic who is attacked, not the conditions they highlight. This is especially prevalent in modern workplaces, where coaching, appreciative inquiry, self-development courses and staff appraisals have long been deployed to deflect criticism.

Criticism is uncomfortable because it calls into question established truths and things we take for granted. As such, the critic, rather than the object of their critique, is made the problem. Not only is it potentially disempowering to stifle legitimate criticism in this way, but we also run the risk of dumbing everything down if we aren't allowed to point a critical finger at things that warrant criticism. However, we also run the opposite risk – of criticism becoming lazy and knee-jerk, of everything being seen as bad or wrong because it's part of 'capitalism', 'instrumentalisation', 'structural racism' or other forms of external oppression. Public debate appears to be caught between these two extremes. One side wants to stifle criticism because it is perceived as unproductive, while the other automates it without thinking critically about the quality of the points being made. For example, it's possible for even a privileged white man to be right about something. Not that these characteristics should automatically confer benefits in terms of argumentation – but nor should the opposite be the case. Good arguments are good regardless of the colour or sex of the person making them.

In addition to in-depth analyses such as Willig's, numerous critical-thinking manuals have been published, and many of them are excellent. They differ from the existential perspective of this book on thoughtfulness, but it is important to mention them, as they can help readers distinguish good arguments from bad, and perhaps even pave the way for a much-needed rational position between the two extremes mentioned above (no criticism versus automatic criticism). In his short and highly accessible manual (in Danish) on critical thinking, the philosopher Christoffer Boserup Skov develops five basic principles for thinking critically: (1) think clearly, (2) eliminate prejudices, (3) think in perspectives, (4) be critical and (5) be able to wonder.[19] They are about finding the most understandable way of expressing our thoughts (without oversimplifying), becoming aware of our own preconceived attitudes, being able to see the world from points of view other than our own, subjecting arguments (not least our own) to closer scrutiny, and maintaining our ability to marvel at the strangeness of the world.

Skov also touches on elementary argumentation theory, i.e. how to distinguish an argument's form from its content. For example, an argument may well be valid without the conclusion being true. Similarly, an argument can have a true conclusion based on invalid reasoning. He mentions an argument that follows the *modus ponens* form:

First premise: If you eat lots of soap, you will grow strong.
Second premise: Agnes eats lots of soap.
Conclusion: Agnes will grow strong.

Validity refers, therefore, to the form of the argument, which in this case is in order. The problem, of course, is that the first premise is false. We might even imagine that the conclusion is actually true – namely that Agnes is growing strong, even if she does eat soap – but that wouldn't be down to the first premise: that you grow strong from eating soap. What the argument lacks is *soundness*, which is achieved when the form is valid, and the premises are true. In such a case, it matters little who makes the argument. The task for the critical thinker is to make the effort to separate the form and content of the argument from the individual making it. Too often, people tend to either agree with an argument because they like the person making it or disagree because they don't. It is useful to practise assessing both the validity of arguments (is the structure in order?) and their soundness (are the premises also true?) in abstraction from who is making them. This is fundamental to critical thinking.

In a similar book in English called *How to Think*,[20] the philosopher Tom Chatfield writes about a number of the fallacies that make us think uncritically. Some of his points are listed below – supplemented by others – for those who want to think critically, in the sense of self-critically, i.e. being critical about their own thinking.

Appeal to emotion: This is a bit tricky because one of this book's basic ideas is that reason and thinking may well be linked to emotions. If we don't understand what it's important to think about – and that invariably involves our emotional life – we can't think in relevant ways. But that doesn't mean an emotional appeal is a good argument per se. From 'I like the Chancellor of the Exchequer', we can't logically conclude 'therefore the budget is really good', nor can we reach the opposite conclusion ('the budget's a disaster because I don't like the Chancellor of the Exchequer'). If a budget is good, it's good for factual reasons related to the economy and public spending, which ultimately has nothing to do with whether or not you like the Chancellor. In a culture based on marketing and spin, citizens, voters and consumers are often manipulated by appeals to the emotions. It's good for the critical thinker to be aware of this strategy – and to think even more critically about what the people you like are saying.

Ad hominem: This is perhaps the most widespread fallacy and closely resembles the appeal to emotions. An ad hominem argument is logically invalid because, in short, it is not aimed at what is said but at who said it. 'You work for the pharmaceutical industry, so we can't trust what you say about the efficacy of vaccines' is an example of an ad hominem argument. It's possible that what is being said about the effectiveness of the vaccines is, in fact, incorrect, but you can't know that based solely on who is making the assertion. Perhaps the most challenging exercise in critical thinking is keeping your eyes on the ball rather than your opponent. An excellent practical exercise is to follow people you disagree with on social media and then assess their positions in light of the arguments put forward, not who they are.

Whataboutery: Whataboutery is the tendency to shift a discussion from what a person has said to a different problem that is perhaps only tangentially related. A common example could be: 'It's pointless to discuss spending cuts by the Left since the Right made huge cuts when it was in power' – or vice versa. No, it is by no means certain that discussing x is pointless simply because y has also happened. Whataboutery is often deployed to relativise statements: 'It may well be that thousands of people have died because of COVID, but what about those who die because of particle pollution?' It may well be the case that particle pollution kills a lot of people, but we can still talk about COVID deaths. And we can talk about particle pollution another time. It may be worth discussing a problem, even when faced with other, bigger ones.

The naturalistic fallacy: In short, this involves claiming something is good just because it is natural. A more general way of expressing the problem is that it involves a move from 'is' to 'ought' – from descriptive statements to normative ones. The eighteenth-century Enlightenment philosopher David Hume ascertained that it isn't logically valid to conclude from a descriptive sentence such as 'God is our Creator' that 'Therefore we ought to obey him'. In purely logical terms, you could just as easily reach the opposite conclusion. But even if we have been aware of this fallacy since Hume, it's still extremely prevalent (for example, 'Changing sex isn't natural – so it's wrong'). Only in cases where an 'ought' is intrinsic to the descriptive statement is it valid to infer something normative. For example, based on the phrase 'she's a bus driver', we might conclude that 'she ought to do what a bus driver ought to do'. This is because 'bus driver' is a functional term that defines a role based on how it is correctly performed (transporting passengers safely from A to B). It would probably be going too far to discuss the details of the naturalistic fallacy in greater depth here, but it's worth noting that the philosophy of virtue I have outlined in this chapter asserts that being human is in itself a functional or normative concept that says something about what the individual human can do if they are a good example of the species. In this way, virtue ethics provides an 'ought' for human beings that avoids the naturalistic fallacy.

False dilemma: This is an either-or fallacy, in which you're presented with a choice between two alternatives that, in reality, aren't mutually exclusive at all. Political rhetoric is full of examples of this ('Either you support us, or you support the terrorists', 'If you don't want to stop all immigration, you're in favour of open borders', etc.). These are expressions of black-and-white thinking that make it hard to find compromises and discern subtle differences. An important element in critical thinking and in the thoughtfulness promulgated in this book is *tolerance of ambiguity* – the ability to see the world from multiple perspectives and accept that not everything is easy to explain. But being tolerant of ambiguity doesn't mean everything is equally valid (to present it that way would in itself be a false dilemma).

Non-sequitur: This is an overarching term for arguments in which a conclusion looks convincing, despite not following from the premise in any logically valid way. Some non-sequitur fallacies are of the anecdotal variety, where we say something general based on a single example ('My grandfather smoked like a chimney his whole life and lived to ninety, so smoking can't be as dangerous as they say'), while others are just conclusions completely detached from the premise ('Linda has a lot of followers on social media. She should be a politician!'). The point, again, is that as a critical thinker you have to practise not only weighing up the truth of a statement, but also whether it actually follows from the premises – regardless of whether or not you like the person making the argument.

Straw man arguments: This is a well-known strategy in which you argue against somebody based on a caricature of their view, making your arguments seem better than theirs. But this is uncritical thinking. Ideally, the critical thinker should seek to turn their opponent into a 'steel man', i.e. present their argument as strongly and convincingly as possible. If you then succeed in rejecting their line of thought, you will have done so on a much firmer basis. Scientific theory also talks of falsification, but in science the process is only applied to relevant and recognised theories, not any old home-spun statements attributable to others. Of course, it can be very difficult to acknowledge that your own pet theory has been falsified. But in the service of the truth it is important that you learn to accept defeat gracefully.

*

According to Chatfield, it's crucial that critical thinkers are aware of what they don't know. The Dunning–Kruger effect, named after the two scientists who demonstrated it, is well known.[21] It is often slightly erroneously presented as the least competent people in a field thinking they know better than their more diligent peers. That is not correct. Rather, the study suggests – although the findings have been subject to considerable scientific debate – that less competent people are more likely to overestimate their abilities. Most people, on the whole, have greater self-esteem than reality justifies, and that is possibly most true of the least able. By now, you know that you should be careful about relying on anecdotal experience. That said, my own observation, based on working at a university for more than two decades, is that the most gifted people are often very concerned with how little they know. The more you know, the more you know about how little you actually know! Less talented people, in turn, are often very concerned with how much they know. The less you know, the less you know about how little you actually know!

I once co-authored a book called *Det, du ikke forstår, gør dig klogere* (What You Don't Understand Makes You Wiser), a title that serves as a neat summary of this chapter. Thinking that generates meaning is about everything we *don't* know – but it often takes a great deal of knowledge to understand how little we actually know. It takes courage to stand by the idea that there's something we don't know, and it takes curiosity to want to learn more. Courage and curiosity can also be examples of virtues that are both ethical and epistemic, as they concern both our actions and our ability to think, which illustrates one of Antiquity's basic philosophical concepts: that the good and the true are two sides of the same coin. Beauty should also be in the picture with the good and the true, which leads us nicely to the subject of the next chapter – the thoughtful life as a beautiful and happy one.

3
Happiness is a thoughtful life

'All happiness is a victory against finitude.'[1] So writes the French philosopher Alain Badiou in his short book on happiness. His idea serves as the starting point for this chapter since, for Badiou, it is precisely thinking that frees us from our finite existence by offering us glimpses of the infinite. He also argues that philosophical thought, in particular, provides us with that opportunity. Badiou's philosophy is a highly individual blend of a typically classical search for the true and absolute (with a penchant for mathematics) going back to Plato as the wellspring of European ideas, and Marx's revolutionary philosophy, which sought to create a better world. He sees capitalism as a force that commodifies human relations and reduces devoted and unconditional love to a quid pro quo transaction. He offers a critique in which capitalism is a threat to everything that is valuable in life, especially love, which he believes is in danger of being swallowed up by an egotistical pleasure project that threatens to make love impossible.

'Our world is marked by speed and lack of coherence', Badiou asserts. As such, he believes philosophy ought to be what allows us to determine, 'through a sort of interruption or caesura of this speed or this incoherence, that *this* is good and *that* is not'.[2] According to Badiou, good and evil transcend arbitrary social constructs, but recognising this requires time to think deeply and coherently. Again, the inspiration from Plato is clear. Badiou believes we've simplified happiness into what he calls 'the semblance of a consumer satisfaction' by following the impulses of instant gratification, the desire for superficial goods and trends. However, true happiness lies in liberation from time – understood as the present, with its accelerating and fragmented culture – and the human finitude that binds us. Directly addressing the reader, Badiou writes: 'Here's what you need to convince you that thinking against opinions and in the service of some truths, far from being the unrewarding and pointless exercise you imagine it to be, is the shortest path to true life, which, when it exists, is signalled by an incomparable happiness.'[3] In other words, a truly happy life consists of thinking critically in the service of truth. It's pure Plato!

Badiou sees happiness, freedom and love as interconnected, and posits that only thinking allows us to understand and embrace this triad. Both love and happiness are based on a form of fidelity, he writes. We misunderstand the nature of freedom if we think it's just about doing what we want. What we want, he stresses, arises from our adaptation to the world. Real freedom is found only in fidelity, in which we must discipline ourselves. Discipline, too, is therefore a precondition for happiness.[4] To achieve true happiness, we must discipline ourselves to transcend time and place – all that which Plato called the world of phenomena. Only those who philosophise can do that, because the philosopher *thinks*, which makes them happier than all those we otherwise imagine are happier: the rich, the powerful, the hedonists, the tyrants. Using thinking to free yourself from time makes both thinking and fidelity to the world possible. We think happiness is being glad and satisfied, being able to consume and enjoy without limits, but these are just coping mechanisms for dealing with life in a thoughtless society. Only through thinking can we rise above all that.

I began this chapter with a dose of Badiou because there is something highly refreshing about a modern philosopher whose thinking is so strikingly out of step with contemporary trends. He dares to think universally, classically – and critically. Another great twentieth-century philosopher, Hannah Arendt, also proposed that thinking can temporarily lift us above and beyond time. She wrote in her diary that 'the me that thinks is ageless; for the experience of thinking time does not exist'.[5] Through thinking, we liberate our experience from the constraints of physical time, in a sense, even from history itself. We can think about the same question in much the same way as Plato and Aristotle. Thoughtfulness allows us to establish a link with them that spans millennia. The thinking self is also liberated from physical time. When I look at the stars and ponder the mystery of living on a tiny planet in a huge universe, there is little difference between my thoughts at age forty-six and those I had at sixteen. I can even gaze at the stars as a middle-aged person and mull over the fact that I looked at exactly the same ones three decades ago, and I marvel at this thought. Our thoughts can roam freely – both backwards and forwards – through personal and collective history. I can also imagine what it would be like to look at the same stars as an old man if I am lucky enough to live to ninety. The Norwegian writer Karl Ove Knausgård describes a similar experience in his essay 'On Spring', in which thinking in a concrete situation frees him from a very everyday event and brings him into contact with an almost platonic eternity. In the following excerpt, Knausgård's daughter's class are having a party:

> I remained where I was, standing with one hand in my pocket and the other on the handle of the pram. The triviality of the ketchup and mustard bottles, the blackened hot dogs, the camping table where the soft drinks were lined up, was almost inconceivable there beneath the stars, in the dancing light of the bonfire. It was as if I was standing in a banal world and gazing into a magical one, as if our lives played out in the borderland between two parallel realities.

> We come from far away, from terrifying beauty, for a newborn child who opens its eyes for the first time, is like a star, is like a sun, but we live our lives amid pettiness and stupidity, in the world of burned hot dogs and wobbly camping tables. The great and terrifying beauty does not abandon us, it is there all the time, in everything that is always the same, in the sun and the stars, in the bonfire and the darkness, in the blue carpet of flowers beneath the tree. It is of no use to us, it is too big for us, but we can look at it, and we can bow before it.[6]

It's a highly romantic idea that we can break through to a more authentic reality, but I don't think Knausgård's point is that life with his daughter and sausages is unimportant. At least, that certainly isn't my point. Rather, it is that in principle and at any time, thoughtfulness can generate wonder, awe and Badiouan happiness, when it liberates us briefly from time and ourselves.

The American philosopher Harry Frankfurt formulated a similar idea. Like Badiou, he compared thinking with love because both can take us beyond ourselves and allow us to rise above the trivialities of everyday life. It is simply a matter of caring about something other than ourselves, which is an expression of love made possible by thoughtfulness. Frankfurt writes that we are at our best as human beings when we 'escape ourselves' through reason or love. By thinking and using reason – which is impersonal because it is something we all share – we can break out of the prison of subjectivity and self-absorption, just as we can through forms of love that are relational and outward-looking. These are ways of caring about something, in which we surrender, so to speak, to something else – for example, the better argument or the beloved other. However, this necessarily carries the risk of disappointment and defeat. It may turn out that I don't have the better argument or that my beloved will leave me.[7] This is what philosophy is about – breaking down the ego and finding joy in knowledge for its own sake. For a true philosopher, it isn't a question of being right and basking in the admiration of others, but of seeking the truth.

Thoughtful immersion

> I have argued that intellectual life, properly understood, cultivates a space of retreat within a human being, a place where real reflection takes place. We step back from concerns of practical benefit, personal or public. We withdraw into small rooms, literal or internal. In the space of retreat, where we consider fundamental questions: what human happiness consists of, the origins and nature of the universe, whether human beings are part of nature, and whether and how a truly just community is possible.[8]

So writes Zena Hitz in *Lost in Thought*, one of the recent books that has most influenced my views on a life of thought. For Hitz, an intellectual life is the key to true happiness. While this quote may make it sound like a withdrawn and isolated existence, thoughtful immersion makes us see the world more clearly, so that we can better live together. Through a thoughtful life, she writes, we can find 'a place away from competition and ranking, using and instrumentalising'.[9] The thoughtful life can be a refuge, which places us at a refreshing remove from the world – not as a place to construct illusions or wallow in pure escapism, but, on the contrary, as a place from which we are able to see and understand the world as it is. Hitz subscribes to Aristotle's ideal of the thoughtful or contemplative life as the happiest one possible, both because it allows for the realisation of human nature in the highest sense and, quite simply, because it makes true knowledge possible.

Like Nussbaum, Hitz emphasises that the humanities are particularly central to the thoughtful life, as they offer insight into our blind spots, perhaps most obviously in the great works of literature. Reading Nabokov's *Lolita*, for example, we are confronted with how easy it is to be seduced by an aesthetic view of the world that reduces another human being to an object of pleasure. The sin of the book's narrator, Humbert Humbert, is that he turns the girl Dolores Haze (whom he systematically abuses after taking on the role of her stepfather) into a creature who exists only for his gratification. The gauntlet thrown down by Nabokov to his readers is, therefore, to see through the narrator's attempt to seduce them. The book isn't an erotic novel, as is often claimed, but a moral tale about the importance of being able to reach out to a reality beyond the subjective – one populated, in this instance, by girls like Dolores, who are vulnerable to the cruelty of adults.[10] Dolores is not even allowed to keep her name. Her abuser calls her Lolita.

For Hitz, the world is something we must both escape from and learn to see more clearly – precisely by distancing ourselves from it via the thoughtful life. As Iris Murdoch also pointed out, a fundamental and universal task for human beings is to try to see the world as it is.[11] To see the forest as a forest, and not just as timber. To see the young girl as Dolores Haze, not just as Lolita. To be able to see through our own egotistical fantasies and escape ourselves. This is not only an ethical demand placed on human beings, but also an opportunity to experience a deeper form of happiness, one associated with the thoughtful life. Hitz identifies four key characteristics of the thoughtful life: (1) it offers a place of retreat and reflection; (2) it seeks to turn its back on competition and the struggle for status, power and prestige; (3) it is a source of human dignity; and (4) it opens space for communion between people.[12] Such a life allows us to escape both from the superficial world of chance and competition, and from ourselves as self-absorbed individuals. Hitz suggests two paths towards this. The first is philosophical and contemplative, which is the focus of this book. The second is artistic, in which the thoughtful life is realised through creative endeavour. On the face of it, the former is more introverted and oriented towards the world of ideas and books, while the latter establishes a more direct connection to the world via hobbies with a creative component (playing music, painting, writing, needlework, etc.). However, Hitz also mentions more observational hobbies, such as birdwatching. The joy of informing yourself and becoming immersed in the world for no purpose other than learning more about it is an essential part of the happiness of the thoughtful life.

Happy amateurs

One recent literary portrait of such a life is Eva Tind's novel about Marie Hammer, *Kvinden der samlede verden* (The Woman Who Joined Up the World).[13] Hammer was a scientist with a great passion for natural history. Tind's book is a thoroughly researched account of Hammer, her life and her scientific work, but it is also a highly compelling novel, full of drama and poetry. Hammer was a mother of four, a housewife, and was never employed by a university, but her unpaid work as a zoologist included identifying 1,000 new subspecies of moss mite. She was part of Knud Rasmussen's Thule Expedition in 1932, made countless other trips overseas, and her work helped substantiate the controversial theory of continental drift (i.e. that all of the Earth's modern continents once formed a single, vast landmass – hence the title of Tind's book).

In addition to telling a compelling story of a life in science, Tind beautifully captures Hammer's joy at learning through research and thoughtful immersion. Hammer started out studying chemistry, physics and botany. Tind writes: 'Marie loves to study things under the microscope. It is as if the invisible worlds of nature are revealed. Through the eyepieces, she sees things no one else sees. The vast open landscape that the world suddenly is. The existence of this wondrous world gives her the biggest rush.' Later, Hammer hears from her fellow student Thorssen, with whom she is in love: "'I'm fascinated by how wind currents move around the Earth. The air you are breathing now was on the other side of the planet five days ago. The oxygen that an African plant exhaled yesterday, you breathe in today, the oxygen binds in your blood and in that way the plant lives on in you", he says. "Just by describing what's actually happening, you realise that everything is connected."'[14] The last sentence could sum up the philosophy of Aristotle, Murdoch and Hitz. Just by describing what is actually happening, you realise that everything is connected – and in realising this, Hammer experiences the thrill of discovery, the thrill of knowing that this wondrous world exists.

One of the last paragraphs of the book is taken from Marie's diary, dated 1981, when she was in her seventies: 'My vision is now so impaired that I realise I have to stop my work. I have spent almost fifty years on my little creatures. Without them, my life is worthless.'[15] Marie Hammer's life was one of immersion in a world outside herself, but also one that required a great deal of courage and perseverance, as well as time and space to think. The beauty of the story lies in its purity. Hammer is almost entirely motivated by the pursuit of knowledge for its own sake. She did not become rich or famous in her lifetime by studying moss mites and natural science. Only later – mainly after Tind's book resurrected her memory – was Hammer accorded the recognition she deserves. As a scientist, she was an amateur, in the original sense (from the French *amateur*, which originally meant lover). Nowadays, the term is often used pejoratively to refer to someone who is just not very good in their field, but Hammer was an amateur in the true sense of a person who loves what they do and is not motivated by money and prestige.

Many people these days are professional thinkers, earning a living from their intellectual endeavours: people who work with communication, branding, idea development, symbol manipulation and so on. While there's nothing wrong with that (I do it myself), we also need to appreciate people like Hammer, who are driven by a love of knowledge, and who practise thinking and immersion as a way of life with intrinsic value. The anthropologist Tim Ingold celebrates amateurs in an inspiring essay. He cites literary scholar Edward Said's definition of amateurism, which is in some ways close to this book's approach to thoughtfulness. According to Said, amateurism is an expression of 'the desire to be moved not by profit or reward but by love for and unquenchable interest in the larger picture, in making connections across lines and barriers, in refusing to be tied down to a specialty, in caring for ideas and values despite the restrictions of a profession'.[16]

Ingold also reflects on his long career, in which he has seen the role of the professional academic change from being a kind of custodian of collective, public knowledge to now being an exerciser of technical expertise in very narrow fields. That is precisely why we need amateurs, he argues, because they understand that real learning – or scholarship – cannot be separated from life itself, and often takes place in private. Of course, we can and should also think along with other people – in conversations and inspiring meetings – but withdrawing to some kind of refuge may also be necessary. According to psychologist Sherry Turkle, one of the foremost researchers on the impact of computers on human consciousness: 'It is only when we are alone with our thoughts – not reacting to external stimuli – that we engage that part of the brain's infrastructure devoted to building up a sense of our stable autobiographical past. [. . .] When we let our minds wander, we set our brains free.'[17] It is not only philosophers such as Plato and Badiou who have stressed how the thoughtful life, or thinking for the sake of thinking, is key to happiness. Numerous empirical studies have reached the same conclusion. For example, in one major study, the social scientists Bryson and MacKerron asked a large number of people with smartphones to install a specially designed app, which allowed the researchers to ask them, at random times during the day, simple questions such as: 'What are you doing just now?' and 'How happy are you right now?'[18] Out of some forty possible activities, none were specifically labelled 'thinking', but it is notable that the activities that made people happiest shared the same feature – they all had inherent or intrinsic value. The top scorer was intimacy and lovemaking, followed by theatre, concerts, museums, sport, gardening, singing, conversations and other things that people usually do for no external purpose. By contrast, the participants were least happy when the activities were instrumental – done to achieve some other purpose. The study found that people were unhappiest of all when in bed sick (after all, you only do that to get better).

But for me, the most surprising result was that people were second-most unhappy while working. People were actually happier commuting, queuing or doing housework than when at their day jobs, which is quite a thought. The implication is that the activities that make thoughtfulness possible – dwelling on the world or nature, being artistic – spark the greatest joy. We are happiest when allowed to be amateurs, which is probably when our *daimon* finds it easiest to speak up and help us reach a state of *eudaimonia* – a full life.

Thought experiment 4: The experience machine

If the analysis presented in this chapter is correct – that there is a deep happiness in a thoughtful life that offers at least temporary release from all sorts of external stimuli and demands – then it is thought-provoking how much of modern life is highly stimulated, especially by the entertainment industry, the internet and other digital technologies.

That is why I have drawn the thought experiment in this chapter from the philosopher Robert Nozick, whose 1974 book *Anarchy, State and Utopia* presents a philosophical fantasy that, despite its science-fiction form, is not terribly far from the world we are actually creating at the moment.[19] I have written about this experiment before[20] and take the liberty of revisiting it here, as it is among the most interesting and controversial thought experiments in the history of philosophy.

Imagine that scientists have invented an experience machine – a supercomputer that plugs into the central nervous system via a sophisticated interface. When plugged into the machine, people experience what makes them most happy and contented. The computer can be programmed to suit the individual. A football fan can play for his country, win the World Cup and go on to be a successful manager of the national team. Someone else might be a world-famous concert pianist or win the Nobel Prize for curing cancer. Or, at least, they *experience* these things. The point is that the experience is so lifelike they don't question the reality of it. Once plugged in, they forget they're linked to the machine. The process is also so complex that it can't be reversed; once plugged in, they can't be unplugged again. Once in the machine, they're always in it – but they're guaranteed the most eventful and pleasurable life possible.

The question is whether we would want to be plugged into a machine like that. Anyone who has seen the *Matrix* films (a science-fiction dystopia in which human beings serve as biological batteries for a supercomputer, which in return feeds the humans with experiences) will be familiar with the fantasy. Pessimists might argue that, in our media society, which constantly stimulates us through the internet and television, we already live in an enormous, collective experience machine. But it's still possible to go for a walk in the woods without our smartphones – unlike if we were plugged into Nozick's machine, which is always on.

Personally, I know that I would never sign up for the machine. But why not, when it guarantees a long and exciting life? One argument I often hear is that we need to have encountered hardship and misfortune to appreciate good fortune and happiness, whereas the machine provides only happiness. But this isn't a valid objection because the machine could be programmed to deliver an optimal balance between good fortune and misfortune, misery and happiness, in a way that maximises the latter. I think a better reason to say no is that the machine only delivers the *experience* of living. It may deliver maximum happiness – understood as the experience of positive emotions and appealing events – but it has no meaning, because it offers no real opportunity to act (only the experience of acting). The machine provides subjective enjoyment, but not the opportunity to do anything that might help us realise more objective human values.

Perhaps this experiment reminds us that there is a difference between living a life and merely experiencing one. The machine only permits the latter. The very point of it is to provide enjoyment and satisfaction, a bit like what Humbert Humbert sought in the way he related to Dolores Haze (whom he calls Lolita). It doesn't matter what the world is like, or how the girl feels, as long as the result is a semblance of enjoyment. But perhaps there is something unfulfilling about trying to reduce reality to the way in which it looks to me subjectively in my experience of life.

If the sources cited in this chapter are correct, there is a more profound happiness than subjective experience, namely engaging with aspects of reality that offer more than their effect on the individual. Marie Hammer immersed herself in the life and characteristics of moss mites. Her work would not have been the same had she experienced them purely subjectively. It is important to accept that the wondrous world exists. All that Nozick's machine offers is the opportunity to experience doing something, but people tend to want more than subjective experiences and to relate to something more real. This is very much in line with Plato's thinking: we want to go beyond the phenomena (or experiences) and approach a more actual reality. We can do this by immersing ourselves in observing moss mites, as they represent something completely different from us, but we can also do it by thinking, by reaching beyond the ephemeral and enjoying a glimpse of the infinite, as Badiou might put it.

I know that I would rather live an authentic life, even if it involves the risk of more suffering, loss and defeat, than merely experience the semblance of a life served up by Nozick's machine. Which would you prefer? And would it be for the same reasons?

4

Thinking as formation

It's time for a break and to take stock of the arguments. I have tried to do three things so far: home in on the essence of different forms of thinking; problematise the age we live in, which in many ways might be called thoughtless; and argue that there is a deep happiness to be found in thoughtfulness. The thoughtful life is one in which immersion is joyful, but also hopefully one in which thinking results in actions that are beneficial for and bring joy to others. Since ancient Greece, the history of European ideas has straddled a schism between the thoughtful life (often referred to as the contemplative life) and the active life, which involves taking part in politics and focusing on collective issues. At their core, are human beings thinking or acting creatures? Are we contemplative or political?

Hannah Arendt, in particular, perpetuated this distinction, but also tried to show that human life ought to encompass both dimensions. Perhaps they are, in fact, deeply connected, in that participating in politics is irrelevant – or even downright dangerous – without critical thinking, which often presupposes a certain distance from the matter at hand. Similarly, thoughtful contemplation can be quickly reduced to a kind of wellness, as in certain forms of meditation, unless it is coupled with a more outward-looking activity and commitment. During certain periods of our lives, one dimension may be more dominant than the other. Older people, for example, may look back on their life and have no desire to do anything political, but their reflections may nevertheless be instructive and inspiring to the young. Conversely, younger people may feel more compelled to be politically active, which may well be commendable, but if they go down that path without due consideration and personal reflection, they risk being swept up in a mob mentality and the associated pitfalls of crowd psychology. Striking a balance between these two dimensions requires formation, which is the main theme of this chapter. Formation can be defined as the process that recreates the opportunity for thoughtfulness and a full life – even in a relatively thoughtless age.

Live less, think more

The tongue-in-cheek title of this section is a nod to psychologist Pia Callesen's bestseller *Live More, Think Less*.[1] The book is a guide to metacognitive psychotherapy, which seems like a reasonable and effective approach to helping people who suffer from depression. In brief, it consists of trying to let go of your worries: the depressed person thinks too much and acts too little, which is no good for anybody. But for those of us who *don't* suffer from depression – who, admittedly, appear to be ever fewer in number – I think there is just as good reason to go in the opposite direction. In other words, perhaps we should think *more*, and live a little *less*. It's not that I want to limit people's opportunities in life or invite them to overthink – some people undoubtedly do think too much about their problems – but I think we can benefit from reflecting on whether 'more' of everything necessarily means 'better'. Do we live better because we live more? Reflecting on this is vital in a culture like ours, in which we are bombarded with calls to do even more, even faster, for even longer. We routinely bandy about that tiny word 'even', especially when politicians or senior managers want us to do something 'even better'. It is no longer good enough to do something well. Everything must constantly be better – or indeed, 'even better'. This is where my defence of thoughtfulness may be relevant to the discussion of depression. It is no coincidence that the sales slogan for the antidepressant 'happy pill' Paxil was: 'Do more, feel better, live longer'.[2] And think less?

The causal relationships are not easy to identify, but it's likely that at least some of the depression that marks our era is a consequence of the ubiquitous demand that we be flexible, innovative, active, agile, mobile, entrepreneurial, self-optimising and engaged in lifelong learning. There are precious few spaces left in which we are exempt from such demands. In his major study of depression and society, the sociologist Alain Ehrenberg argues that the high incidence of depression in the West is an inevitable consequence of the fatigue and exhaustion arising from these endless demands for *more*.[3] In particular, people are exhausted by the demand that we must do more about the *self*. The self has become the most important resource on which we need to do some work. We saw the same concern in Heidegger, who analysed modern human beings' technological and instrumental relationship with themselves. Ehrenberg's *Weariness of the Self: Diagnosing the History of Depression in the Contemporary Age* is about precisely this need to optimise and develop ourselves throughout our lives, to be authentic, socially adept and emotionally capable. With all its personal, cognitive, emotional and social competencies, the self has become material that must be endlessly exploited – not least by the individual. So, might one source of the worries of those with depression perhaps be that they (rightly?) fear being too slow and backward-looking in an age infatuated with speed and the future? It's all just so exhausting. But the cure may not simply consist of thinking less and living more, as Callesen says, but rather in thinking *more* – and more *critically* – about the basic conditions under which we live our lives. If finding a little more time and peace for reflection means that we live a little less, then so be it. That would probably be good for all of us – including those with depression.

Earlier in the book, I sought to analyse the critical thinking and thoughtfulness that may be necessary counterweights to some of the problematic aspects of our age. I will now spend the rest of this chapter linking it to the concept of formation because there is a fundamental connection between formation and thoughtfulness. I don't claim to be able to capture all aspects of formation by linking it to thinking, of course, because formation is certainly not just a matter of thinking. It is also about the body and practical skills. But, as we will see in the next chapter, even these are often connected to thinking. Nevertheless, I believe that thinking is an essential element of what we call formation. I will argue for this by again picking up the thread from Aristotle to Hannah Arendt, who proposed that thoughtfulness is a particularly important form of human existence.

Rising up to humanity

At this point, I might as well reveal my own position on formation. Of course, there are myriad definitions, theories and traditions regarding the concept, and my task here is not to review them all. So let me say very briefly that I subscribe to the philosopher Hans-Georg Gadamer's general approach, which builds on German and Greek philosophy. He succinctly outlines his understanding of formation in a snappy slogan: *rising up to humanity through culture*.[4]

This definition of formation is based on three key concepts: rising up, humanity and culture. The most important of these is probably the word in the middle: humanity. Formation thinking, which runs like a red thread from the ancient Greek idea of *paideia* to Gadamer in the twentieth century, is based on the idea of humanity as a process of becoming – something that is neither merely there, nor unfolds by itself. Instead, humanity – whatever it is – is something we must *cultivate*. This requires *paideia*, which can be translated as upbringing, teaching or formation, and is the etymological root of the word 'pedagogy'. Pedagogy is a practice of cultivation in which new generations are introduced to their culture and encouraged to think independently and critically about it. As we noted in Chapter 1, in German it is called *Bildung*.

This notion of pedagogy as cultivation brings us to the next key concept: culture. To my mind, culture should not be understood as consisting of causal forces that externally influence people, but as forms of life in which you participate and are brought up. The concept of culture is highly complex. Here, however, it simply serves as a reminder that formation always takes place within a cultural context. If there is such a thing as general humanity – if humanity has common features – then it is self-evident that there are also countless cultural paths to its realisation. Rising up to humanity doesn't happen in the same way in a modern Danish state school as it did in the hunter-gatherer cultures of old when the young gradually learned to participate in the tribe's most important activities. But the assertion is that there is always a common humanity that can be realised through cultural processes.

Rising up, the third key concept, appears to be almost synonymous with upbringing. To be raised up is to be elevated, to be enlightened. It can also be used in the sense of ascending from the position of learner. Educational thinking is full of such vertical metaphors, all of which are, of course, linked to the bodily experience of being able to see more when we stand up. Or it may simply be a matter of growing and gaining an increasingly broad view from a higher vantage point. Formation is a process of growth that isn't based on consuming proteins and carbohydrates but on absorbing cultural works, traditions and practices. The outcome of this process is that, at some point, we come of age and are able to think independently and make up our own minds.

If formation is rising up to humanity through culture, then the concept can be said to be the opposite of other contemporary development concepts, which are linked more to the individual – self-development, skills enhancement, self-optimisation, personal development, self-realisation and all the others of the same ilk. These concepts imply that the individual has a unique core, a set of signature strengths (as they say in positive psychology), special competencies, learning styles or intelligences, which must be realised to the fullest extent possible. In short, self-development is about becoming yourself. It may even be about becoming 'the best version of yourself', to use the modern vernacular. This is a movement from the internal to the external. In other words, we have an inner potential that must be brought out – possibly with the help of a coach, manager, mentor, supervisor or therapist.

In the words of the sociologist Andreas Reckwitz, self-development is, in that sense, a singular process in which we are individuated to the greatest possible extent – and, most importantly, through which we become authentic.[5] Reckwitz analysed the entire development of modernity, framing it as a story of how this process of singularisation affects everything from the economy and working life to culture, lifestyle and politics. Singularisation means less emphasis on the general and the universally human, and more on the particular, the unique, the different, the extraordinary, the authentic, the special. Reckwitz doesn't specifically discuss formation or thinking, but, based on his analysis, it would be no surprise if all of this singularisation were to marginalise a more general concept of formation. Reckwitz writes that we are in a crisis of generality to such an extent that it has become odious even to mention the idea of (a shared) human nature. We no longer talk about or on behalf of the general, because to do so is to forget that 'we are all unique' (as we often hear) and that belonging to certain groups and subcultures gives rise to special ways of experiencing the world, which is where 'identity politics' begins. These two starting points – the purely individual and unique on the one hand, identity-based group affiliation on the other – appear incompatible, which makes it difficult to talk about formation in the sense of rising up to humanity. When we doubt or deny the possibility of a general humanity we end up with, at best, singularised conceptions of formation, which crystallise in, for example, the concept of self-formation, in which we are formed through our encounters with the communities we select and with which we share tastes (musical subcultures, for example).[6]

In my own work, I have long wanted to resurrect the idea of the universally human, and I have argued that formation towards this end must take precedence over singularised self-development.[7] That is not to say that I would deny that we are all unique individuals, or that we all belong to particular groups, communities and nations that shape our identity and to which we have a sense of belonging. But I think there is good reason to bear in mind the classic dictum, jointly coined by the anthropologist Clyde Kluckhohn and the psychologist Henry Murray, that all people are at one and the same time like everyone else, like some others and like no one else.[8] And we must include thinking about all of these dimensions in our lives.

This means, firstly, that we are all simply human. Biology determines us as *Homo sapiens* and philosophy (at least Aristotle's) as *zoon logikon*. Under both designations, thinking is the key characteristic of our common humanity. Becoming human means realising our potential to become thinking beings. We are, in a real sense, the only creatures with that potential. Secondly, it means that we all have a language, a gender, a culture and much more – but not a whole host of other mother tongues, genders, etc. We are like some others, and that endows us with an identity, because it gives us someone and something with which to identify. And thirdly, it means that we each have unique life stories, relationships and obligations, because we are exactly who we are as individuals. Only I am me and I am like no other. This same applies to our thinking: part of my thinking is entirely my own, because only I have unique, first-hand knowledge of my own history. Like everyone else, I also have a unique way of thinking, but a large part of my thinking comes from others with whom I share a language, culture and way of life. If there is a general ability to think that belongs to humanity, there must also be universal norms for good thinking – and perhaps eternal questions on which we might dwell thoughtfully. This was, in a way, the Greeks' great gift to the subsequent millennia: to formulate the (philosophical) questions that all of us can discuss thoughtfully, regardless of whether we were born today or a thousand years ago, regardless of our gender, nationality or faith. Of course, we may approach these questions in different ways and arrive at different answers. But that is precisely the point: our thinking is at one and the same time like everyone else's, some other people's and no one else's.

A great deal of contemporary self-development focuses almost exclusively on the third part – we are like no one else. Formation thinking, if it is truly to raise us up to humanity, must necessarily also work at the level where we are like everyone else: it is through thinking that we grow to be part of the collective. As mentioned, the Greek name for general human formation was *paideia*, which refers to the set of physical, psychological and cultural abilities and characteristics that we have to acquire as human beings, precisely because all of us are like all other people. My view is that it's all well and good to 'realise yourself' as a unique individual, but not at the expense of the universal human values and obligations from which ethics originate. To put it bluntly, it is fine to be yourself, but not if that means you're a bad person. As Søren Kierkegaard wrote, to be an ethical person presupposes realising the general nature of humanity – without which it is difficult to imagine an ethics at all.[9] Written over the temple of Apollo in Delphi in ancient Greece were the words 'Know thyself' – but this was not intended as a call to find your individual learning style or realise your authentic self. Originally, it was more akin to a demand to understand yourself in terms of your general humanity before you entered the temple – as a mortal being among other mortals, in the face of the sacred and the divine. It is an invitation to a broad concept of human contemplation. I believe there is something edifying and ethical in the idea that a form of equality is an innate part of being human. In other words, in the recognition that we are all created equal, as the American Declaration of Independence puts it. This doesn't mean that all people are equally clever, skilful or inventive, just that we are equal in dignity and worth. That is the basic idea underpinning humanism, which first emerged in an embryonic form in Antiquity, gained momentum during the Renaissance and the Enlightenment, but now risks being challenged if we question the idea of common humanity.

To think is to live

Let us return to the question of the role *thinking* can play in rising up to humanity through culture. How is thinking related to formation? Throughout the book, I have followed a thread leading back to the philosophy of Plato and Aristotle. The ancient Greeks had a teleological view, in which the world and its processes were seen via the lens of purpose (*telos* in Greek). In terms of the nature of the physical world, this is, of course, an outmoded worldview. But perhaps it still provides an indispensable insight into the nature of humanity. We now know that stones fall to the ground and fire rises to the sky due to forces of nature, whereas Aristotle believed that the stone sought out the ground and fire the sun because that was where they belonged. Aristotle saw striving, meaning and intention in the movements of everything, an approach that suffered a setback with modern, mechanical natural science (as conceived by Galileo, Newton and others), which demystified the world from the Renaissance onwards. The actions of human beings were also subsequently demystified, as the modern understanding of humankind – as expressed, for example, through the emergence of psychology in the eighteenth and nineteenth centuries – was based on causal explanations of human behaviour. Psychology modelled itself on mechanical physics, most clearly in behaviourism, which considered our behaviour as just the blind consequence of reward and punishment, but also in aspects of later neuroscience and cognitive science. Humans and their manifestations of life were reduced to mechanical movements in time and space because it was thought that this was the only way a science of psychology could proceed. But humans aren't fire or stone and can't be understood in terms of cause and effect in the same way because their actions are also guided by intentions and human nature. Fire and stone don't strive for anything. People do. For that reason, we can still derive a great deal of benefit from reading Aristotle's psychology and ethics, which describe and analyse this striving human nature, even though his views on physics are massively outdated.

It was the legacy from Aristotle that Hannah Arendt addressed in her final (unfinished) work, arguably her magnum opus, *The Life of the Mind*.[10] Arendt, one of the greatest modern thinkers, died in 1975 while working on the book, which was published a few years later. In it, she set out to analyse the three basic functions of the life of the mind: thinking, willing and judging. Although she only completed her analyses of the first two, the book still offers a deep understanding of thinking in particular. In the introduction to the Danish translation, the recently deceased historian of ideas Hans-Jørgen Schanz describes some of the impulses that lay behind the book. On the one hand, Arendt wanted to complete her work in philosophical anthropology that began with *The Human Condition*, which focused on the active life of humans.[11] There the emphasis was on work, production and action – in other words, everything that Aristotle assigned to the realm of practical reason. In *The Life of the Mind*, this perspective is supplemented with an in-depth analysis of the contemplative life, with an emphasis on thinking or theoretical reason. The latter focus resurrects what Aristotle called *theoria*, i.e. philosophical activity that is oriented not towards external goals such as practice or production, but to meaning and truth per se.

Another reason Arendt focused on thinking was that she wanted to explain her understanding of the Nazi war criminal Adolf Eichmann, as described in her famous work on his trial, in which she introduced the controversial concept of the banality of evil.[12] Eichmann was one of the principal architects behind the Nazi regime's mass murder of the Jewish people in Europe. Arendt provoked readers by describing the nature of his evil as banal because he didn't appear to be a sadistic monster. Eichmann claimed he was just following orders. He even quoted the duty ethics of Immanuel Kant approvingly, despite his actions being anything but Kantian. Nonetheless, Arendt wanted to explain her analysis that Eichmann had been, in the truest sense, thoughtless. In Arendt's eyes, evil is an expression of thoughtlessness and, therefore, banal. Eichmann may well have been, in a sense, highly gifted, but Arendt was interested in a kind of formation-based thinking, which is independent of intellectual acumen. In Arendt's sense, thinking includes conscience, in the form of attention and thoughtfulness towards other people. This was an attribute sorely lacking in Eichmann, who had turned himself into an unthinking cog in a machine, obeying orders. You can, of course, have a high IQ without thinking very much in Arendt's sense of the word – and vice versa.

One of the most important distinctions in *The Life of the Mind* is between thinking and knowing. Arendt writes that the goal of the former is meaning, while the goal of the latter is knowledge. This is a somewhat idiosyncratic use of these terms, but in using them, she establishes a link to Kant's distinction between reason and understanding. Understanding is linked to the world of experience, in which sensory impressions are connected to concepts and provide knowledge. We need this kind of knowledge in order to survive and conduct ourselves. For example, what is that on the forest floor – a snake or a branch? If we go for a walk in the woods, it would be useful to know how to distinguish between the two, and we do so by drawing on our understanding. Thinking is not directly useful in the same way, because its goal is meaning. In other words, it is an activity done for its own sake, because meaning has no goal other than meaning.

I described this earlier in the book when discussing how thinking aimed at generating meaning can have intrinsic value. On this point, Arendt is in line with Kant, as well as with the Greeks. She writes that 'the thinking activity belongs among those *energeiai* which, like flute-playing, have their ends within themselves and leave no tangible outside end product in the world we inhabit'.[13] In the same passage, she refers to the Roman philosopher Cicero, who believed that when we philosophise, i.e. think, we briefly transform into 'mortal gods'. Here, in our finite life, we can glimpse infinity, just as in Badiou's definition of happiness. In many contexts, we – like other animals – are preoccupied with engaging in useful activities that will provide us with food, facilitate reproduction and ensure survival. However, through thinking, we can, even just for a moment, rise above these instrumental matters and simply watch and reflect, which is deeply meaningful in itself. Arendt notes the etymological connection between the word theory (derived from *theos*) and the divine. To theorise and think philosophically is temporarily to adopt a divine view of the world. This is also supposedly the origin of the word *theatre*. When we are able to think and philosophise, we view the world as if we are gods in a theatre. That is true happiness.

Achieving this requires a contemplative way of life that frees us from work, production and consumption – not as a permanent state of being, but from time to time. This liberation was called *schole agein* in Greek, and is the origin of the concept of school, which basically means 'free time'. It is this free time that makes possible the process of formation in a life that 'stems from the meeting between the thing when it is taken out of use, and the person when they are taken out of their function'.[14] It arises when the thing is not defined by its utility value ('what can we use mathematics for?'), and the person is not defined by their role, be it as a man, a woman, a wage-earner or a football fan. Formation can be understood as linked to 'the processes that take place in and stem from such suspended states, where humans connect with aspects of culture and nature'.[15] Formation can, therefore, take place when ordinary instrumental agendas and opportunistic motives are abolished, allowing us freely and vividly to engage in what Arendt calls 'non-cognitive thinking'. She writes that this kind of thinking consists of admiration, confirmation and approval, which lead to the formation of meaning – and that speech is a prerequisite for this whole process. Thinking can't exist without speech, as the activities of the mind manifest through words. Formation can only happen when people talk to each other in a real and meaningful sense, rather than try to persuade each other. Speech allows us to detach ourselves from our animalistic bonds to the useful and opportune and instead exchange thoughts and ideas for no purpose other than to generate meaning. In short, thinking comes from speech, which in turn comes from conversation, i.e. speaking together. People learn to talk through speaking to others, which is also how we learn to think.

However, speech and thinking can also be part of our inner life – although probably not initially. As developmental psychology has demonstrated, we acquire language in conversation with others (more on that in the next chapter). But once we learn to speak, we can also talk to ourselves without making our words public. Of course, it can be problematic if our inner dialogue is judgemental or forever finding faults (as is often the case with people with depression, who often have negative thoughts about themselves). On the other hand, it can also be wonderful, as inner dialogue can lead people to meaningful new insights or enable them to dwell on treasured memories. Here, Arendt pays tribute to Socrates, whom she credits with the discovery that you not only talk to others, but also to yourself.[16] As previously mentioned, Socrates was famous for suddenly falling into a reverie and seeming to be preoccupied with his own inner life for a long time. In fact, he was conversing with his *daimon*, which in Greek means fate, conscience and the inner voice. Afterwards, he would return to the outer, active life in the company of others. This is an almost perfect illustration of the alternating relationship between the contemplative and the active life.

One of the premises of this book is that Socratic thoughtfulness can be considered Western philosophy's version of Eastern meditation practice. In modern times, meditation has become mindfulness, which can be learned as a technique at night school or on a personal development course with colleagues. While mindfulness, according to the professionals, consists of being attentively present and simply registering the impressions you receive in a non-judgemental way, thoughtfulness is a more active process to which you are committed. Simply put, mindfulness is about thinking and pondering less, while thoughtfulness is about thinking and pondering more. However, we should probably be careful not to position them as polar opposites. Although I have written here about 'living less and thinking more', Aristotle and Arendt make it clear that thinking is also a potent – and indeed, very much alive – form of activity: If we don't think, we cut ourselves off from the life of the mind. We become sleepwalkers. To think is to be spiritually awake. To think is to live.

Arendt also writes about thinking and life: 'If thinking is an activity that is its own end and if the only adequate metaphor for it, drawn from our ordinary sense experience, is the sensation of being alive, then it follows that all questions concerning the aim or purpose of thinking are as unanswerable as questions about the aim or purpose of life.'[17] In other words, thinking is an activity, a way of living. It is probably something that people have always practised (or at least described) since the ancient Greeks. It is handed down through generations and continuously taken up anew. However, Arendt believed that this tradition was, unfortunately, waning along with our general awareness of the importance of the past: 'What has been lost is the continuity of the past as it seemed to be handed down from generation to generation.'[18] Not long ago, we even reached a point where opportunism itself could be heralded as a kind of ideal for formation,[19] which is almost as far from the Aristotle–Arendt line as you can get. By means of pedagogy and education, the 'competitive state' is supposed to create 'opportunistic individuals'. The idea is to motivate individuals to think of themselves as 'responsible for their own competencies and for their own development', as the political scientist Ove Kaj Pedersen wrote ten years ago in his book about the competitive state.[20] Formation – rising up to humanity through culture – is the very opposite of opportunism. It is about understanding the world and life without (and raised above) instrumental calculations of utility and it presupposes the ability to think, which is under pressure.

In other words, the *Zeitgeist* makes thinking and formation difficult. As described in Chapter 3, the result of the modern technological approach to life is that people are now understood as entrepreneurial beings, existing in a world of resources they must exploit and control as far as possible. We seek ever greater flexibility and efficiency for its own sake in pursuit of the overall goal of optimisation.[21] But the alternative to approaching the world through control, mastery

Thinking as formation 83

and optimisation is to approach it with curiosity – playfully, receptively, gratefully. Arendt makes two important points about this: that thinking is the same as giving thanks (and not just etymologically, in the German *denken* and *danken*), and that 'solitary thinking in itself constitutes the only relevant action in the factual record of history'.[22] Regarding the first, I agree, at least if we understand 'thinking' as the contemplative activity handed down from Socrates and Aristotle to Arendt. In other words, thinking that is without purpose, that generates meaning, is closely linked to gratitude for that about which the individual is thinking, and to conscience, care and concern (which Heidegger called *Sorge*). We saw this, for example, in Marie Hammer, who was careful and caring in her work with the moss mites. The book about her life expresses an elementary gratitude that these beings exist. As for the second point, solitary thinking is perhaps meaningful enough (again, think Socrates and his *daimon*), but it is only possible because we have first learned to think along with others (which also applies to Socrates). A *daimon* can only speak because others have given it language.

I don't believe we will re-establish formation simply by focusing on old traditions and masterpieces or drawing up canonical lists of art and culture and telling school students to learn from them. These may be excellent initiatives, but if not accompanied by thinking – as a free and meaningful activity – they will produce nothing but rote learning. Thinking, and therefore formation, can be found in the strangest places, and certainly not only in formal school settings (where we might argue that it faces particularly adverse conditions). The cyclist can think with no external purpose while pedalling away, the artisan while working with tools and materials. Places that offer opportunities for play are particularly conducive to thinking because the concept of thinking is closely linked to perceptions of play as an activity that is both joyful and is its own purpose. It has no use as such: it leads us just as much as we lead it, and in collective play our actions regularly surprise us. No matter how well we think we know the game, we can always be surprised by how it turns out. It is the same with thinking. We can surprise ourselves in play and in thinking precisely because there is no expectation to achieve anything other than more play and more thinking. Wherever pure instrumentalism can be abolished – in thinking, in play, in love, in hobbies – the possibility of rising up to humanity through culture arises. The life of the spirit isn't just an intellectual endeavour. We need to identify all of the areas in which we can think more and make room for formation.

Thought experiment 5: Teletransportation

Formation means growing into communities and traditions in order to look after and renew them. Formation is about becoming a human being among other human beings while also learning to think for yourself and speak with your own voice. In this way, formation is crucial to becoming what we usually call a person. A person isn't just a biological organism but an independent being who can be held responsible for their actions and who understands themselves as part of a much bigger story involving others, which unfolds over time. But what is it about the person that makes them stay the same? We know that everything changes, and this also applies to the individual: we grow older, our appearance changes and our body's cells are continuously replaced. Biologically speaking, we change completely, and yet we remain the same person. How is that possible?

One of the oldest and most difficult philosophical conundrums is about identity: What is it that makes something remain the same over time? The Greeks used the riddle of Theseus' ship to illustrate this question. In this thought experiment, a ship sails at sea for many years. Gradually, its planks, oars and rudder wear out and are replaced. Over time, every single component has been changed, and nothing is left of the original vessel. And yet the sailors thought they were sailing on the same ship. Perhaps an object's identity isn't derived from something material (in the simple sense) but from its form.

The problem becomes more complicated and relevant when we talk about people. What makes a person identical to themselves over time and place? We know today that the atoms in our bodies, too, are continuously replaced. Philosophers have long pondered this question, giving rise to interesting thought experiments. One of the most recent and exciting is Derek Parfit's teleportation scenario. Parfit was a brilliant philosopher who wrote only two books in his career, of which *Reasons and Persons* (1984) is considered particularly seminal. It presents the following thought experiment.[23] Parfit imagines a science-fiction world in which some form of teleportation is possible. People can travel to the newly colonised Mars in seconds by entering a teleporter and pressing a button. The machine then scans your entire body and brain. All of the information about the atoms in the organism – their properties and interrelationships – is then sent to Mars at the speed of light, where a replicator produces a complete copy of the person using an advanced 3D printer. This is not simply a matter of genetic similarity, like identical twins. In this case, the copy is in every conceivable way identical to the original. After pressing the button in the teleporter, you wake up – in a sense – in the receiver unit on Mars. The question is, who is the 'you' that wakes up? Which person is that?

In one version of the thought experiment, the original body is destroyed as soon as the button is pressed. This is a problem because the person who occupies the original body might not find dying all that cool, even if a copy is created on Mars. (To make the example a little less dramatic, it could just as easily be a journey from Manchester to Birmingham.) What if you regret pressing the button? What if you start screaming just before your original body is destroyed? Is it any consolation if the technician assures you that you won't die because you will live a healthy life on another planet? According to Parfit, yes, this would be a consolation. He claims that there is nothing sufficiently interesting about personal identity – i.e. what makes a person the same over time – such that we should be concerned about dying in one body and being recreated in another. The only thing that matters is a psychological connection between the two. In other words, the important thing is that you have the same memories, personality and duties and, in every way, have the same relationships to others. For Parfit, there is no soul, nor any other indestructible part of us, which guarantees personal identity. There are only psychological properties, all of which are preserved during the transfer from one place to another. In principle, you could just as well fall asleep on Earth and wake up on Mars, not knowing whether you had travelled very fast and simply slept throughout the journey or if you'd been teleported in a new incarnation.

In another version of the experiment, the original body isn't destroyed but lives on – as does the copy. In principle, the two could meet. If the copy returns to Earth, it could talk to . . . itself. And that's the crux of the matter: Who are *you*? One of these two people, the other, or both? It might seem silly for a philosopher like Parfit to spend time developing and discussing this experiment, but he did so to qualify the debates about who and what we are. Perhaps you've thought about something similar yourself.

Philosophers have had three basic takes on the nature of identity: that we are basically souls, that we are basically bodies, and that we are memories or otherwise constituted by psychological continuity. Parfit advocates the third idea, arguing that what is relevant is neither a spiritual nor a physical identity, but psychological continuity – which need not even be linked to the same body.

Parfit himself considered his philosophical position to be liberating because, in his eyes, it reduced the fear of death. When identity is unimportant – when there is no soul or substantial self that can die – then death is simply the cessation of experiences for me as an individual. Fortunately, there will be many other experiences, some of which will perhaps even be influenced by my actions (for example, my children's lives) or by ideas I have conveyed (for example, through a book like this one). I don't know that I find quite the same comfort as Parfit in abandoning the idea of personal identity, but he nonetheless expressed his thoughts beautifully in this passage, which was widely shared after his death in 2017:

> When I believed [that personal identity is what matters], I seemed imprisoned in myself. My life seemed like a glass tunnel through which I was moving faster every year, and at the end of which there was darkness. When I changed my view, the walls of my glass tunnel disappeared. I now live in the open air. There is still a difference between my life and other people's lives. But the difference is less. Other people are closer. I am less concerned about the rest of my life, and more concerned about the lives of others.[24]

The quotation beautifully illustrates how philosophical reflection can lead to existential change. Thoughtful reflection on personal identity can lead to a freer life. In the quote, Parfit also touches on the ethical consequences of abandoning the strongly embedded idea of personal identity. When the substantial self disappears, it becomes more difficult to defend selfish actions. It doesn't matter so much whether it is me or others who have certain experiences. The most important thing is that someone has them. If I refuse to give money to those in need because I'd rather go on a summer holiday to the Maldives, I am putting my future 'summer-holiday self' above the current predicament of others. And why would I want to do that? If identity isn't important, surely I can't favour my future self, from whom I am separated in time, at the expense of other people around me now, from whom I am separated in space? Based on this kind of thinking, it's little wonder that Parfit's philosophy has been compared to Buddhism. He was a member of Giving What We Can, an organisation that asks people to donate at least 10 per cent of their income to charity.

*

I am not sure Parfit's ideas are directly relevant to the discussion of thinking and formation in this chapter. Perhaps indirectly so? Perhaps formation consists precisely of considering your own (un)importance in relation to the larger communities of which you are part. Formation is understanding that you are only something by virtue of something else *in relation to which* you are formed. If you play around with the teleportation experiment, you might not reach the same conclusion as Parfit. I would probably be so self-absorbed that I'd be reluctant to die in one module for a copy of me to live on in the other (except that Parfit would say it's not a copy – it is also me). I am also more concerned with my future self than with so many other selves who live here and now around me. That's why, for example, I'm saving for my pension and not everyone else's. However, Parfit's ideas are nevertheless a stone in my philosophical shoe. We may well need thinking like his if we are to be sufficiently interested in the lives of future generations. It's worth thinking about.

Back to formation: Individuals without individualism

You may never have thought about the meaning of the word 'formation' before, but if you have, you probably linked the concept to something cultural, maybe learning about classic literature, cooking or furniture design. This form of 'bourgeois education', as some would call it, has little to do with the concept of formation that concerns me here. For Gadamer and thinkers like him, formation is about rising up to humanity. This happens through culture, but culture is an extremely broad concept that can encompass science, the arts, handicrafts or working-class culture. As long as we are dealing with contexts in which the individual learns to face the world, i.e. grows into it, and learns to think better and more deeply about the contexts of which they are part, then it counts as formation. As mentioned earlier, Marie Hammer's life was an example of lifelong formation. Formation abolishes habitual and normative economic and opportunistic logics, and we encounter the world as it is. Being able to think this way is a particularly human trait because other living creatures are largely bound by their instincts, basic survival needs and the desire to reproduce. These biological realities are also, of course, crucial to humans as well, but as a *zoon logikon* we can temporarily suspend instrumentalism and adopt a different, more thoughtful relationship to the world, which has value per se for the type of beings we are.

Formation means accepting existing traditions and practices, caring for them and perpetuating them, but also acquiring the authority to speak with your own voice and adopt independent positions in the contexts of which you are part. Herein lies a contradiction: How can you think for yourself when you are also a product of certain conditions and circumstances? The answer is by transcending current conditions, for example by reflecting on universally human questions – perhaps even eternal ones – that are not exclusively linked to gender, class, culture, society or the individual. I return to Greek philosophy again and again, including in this book, in an attempt to create some distance between us and the age we live in. Once we have acquired the thinking tools of philosophy, we can learn to use them to address all kinds of topical problems. By thinking more deeply about the eternal questions, we can return to the concrete and the local in a more informed way. This has been a basic element in thinking about formation since at least Plato, as seen in his famous allegory of the cave. This journey – from being at home to going out into the world and coming home again – doesn't have to involve a physical trip to Nepal or Brazil – it can be in the mind.

If I may express it somewhat paradoxically, the aim of formation processes in families, institutions and schools is to create a society of individuals without individualism. A fully rounded person is an individual who can think for themselves but also reflect on the circumstances that formed them into that thinking individual. It is someone who knows that they did not create themselves but owe their existence to others as part of a culture that they feel a sense of responsibility for looking after and perpetuating. In that sense, there's no contradiction between individuals and communities that work well. In fact, the former presuppose the latter. It is hard for individuals to exist in unstable or poorly functioning communities because under those circumstances you end up with atomisation, with people being alienated from each other and not feeling they owe each other anything. They become competitors. The fact that Eichmann couldn't think also meant he didn't understand the meaning of the individuality of others. He couldn't comprehend that other people – Jews, disabled people or communists – are like everyone else, someone else and nobody else. Just like him.

5
Where does thinking come from?

Throughout the book, I have returned time and again to the ancient Greek idea of the *daimon*. Among other things, the idea expresses the experience of thoughts coming to us. My thoughts are, of course, *mine*, but they are also experienced as voices and images that come to my mind. They show up. The same applies, incidentally, to speech. When I say something, it is *me* who speaks – but sometimes, I don't quite know what I'm going to say until I hear myself say it. Both our thoughts and our speech can take us by surprise. They are generated by deep processes in the body, brain and central nervous system, based on years of exchanges with parents, partners, children, friends and colleagues. The thoughts also take the form of our experiences of aesthetics, nature, film and music – and, more negatively, of crises, losses and trauma. Our thoughts are also shaped by humankind's long evolutionary history, the adaptation of our organs and bodies to a dangerous world, and generations of experience with waterholes and wild animals. So while it is true that I think my own thoughts, it's also true that they have a life of their own.

A thoughtful life is, therefore, one in which you try to listen to your *daimon* and talk to it in your thinking. A thoughtful life is necessarily dialogical – even when you think without talking to others – because all thinking stems from conversation. The thought experiments that I have proposed in this book are meant as exercises in thoughtfulness, ways to trigger your *daimon* and initiate a conversation with it. Maybe you can speak to friends and acquaintances about the experiments and try thinking together. Or perhaps you might want to go for a walk and think about the various questions raised by the experiments. You might return home with the desire to change your life or reform society. Or maybe you'll decide that most things are fine the way they are.

You might be thinking it's somewhat fantastical to say that thinking comes from a *daimon*. Of course, this is more of a poetic explanation of the origin of thinking than a scientifically satisfactory one. In this chapter, I will offer a slightly more detailed and scientific take on the roots of thinking before rounding off with a discussion of the different dimensions of existence that can bring it to life.

The thinking life and the emotional life

We can split the question of where thinking comes from into two sub-questions: Where does it come from in terms of human evolution? And where does it come from in the individual's own life? The former concerns what's known as *phylogenesis* – how the evolution of the species forms the basis of the ability to think; the latter concerns *ontogenesis* – the development of the individual.

Taking the latter first, the answer is twofold: Thinking comes from original emotions that are regulated by social processes. We feel before we think. Children don't learn to think out of the blue. There has to be something at stake in the child's life that encourages them to think. As described at the start of the book, referring to Dewey, we typically think reflectively when faced with an obstacle, a dilemma or the unexpected. This also applies to children, whose emotions inform them when something important is at stake. But emotions don't arise out of the blue, either. They develop gradually through social interaction, which developmental psychologists sometimes call 'proto-conversation' – a form of conversation that precedes verbal dialogue. As such, thinking requires both emotions and a conversational social life. I will now elucidate that process in a bit more depth.

In recent years, a common thread in psychological research has been the assertion that thoughts and feelings are much more closely linked than previously thought. Many would now say that thinking emerges from emotional life. But how? Many researchers have sought to answer this question, but I will turn to a single source here, the work of psychiatrist Stanley Greenspan and philosophical psychologist Stuart Shanker. In their fascinating book *The First Idea*, they ask the simple but perplexing question: What exactly was the first idea?[1] The book unfolds an evolutionary understanding of how the human species acquired ideas and learned to think, as well as a developmental psychological theory of how the ability to think is acquired during the individual child's life. If their theories are correct, and these are parallel processes, it suggests that a development that took millions of years of evolutionary history now occurs in about two years in an individual child. Their general point is that the ability to think firstly presupposes the ability to use symbols (especially, of course, language); and, secondly, that the ability to symbolise arises from emotions. In other words, emotions lead to symbols, which lead to thinking. Or, schematically:

emotions in relationships → language → thinking

The basic hypothesis is that children are born with a repertoire of emotions that later develop through interaction with their caregivers. This idea has been very well explored in developmental psychology research, which has shown that, virtually from birth, children can both imitate others and mirror adult emotions. For example, if you stick out your tongue to a newborn child, they will often try to 'respond' by sticking out their tongue. Later, when the child masters motor skills and sounds, they may, for example, respond with a 'boo!' when their parent says 'boo!' to them. Both parent and child can amplify each other's emotional state through happy, welcoming facial expressions, mimicry and gestures. This is proto-conversation, in which the child may smile or laugh at the adults, initiating an intimate emotional choreography. It's a form of dialogical emotional regulation that can amplify positive emotions and subdue negative ones. And it's also the starting point for our ethical life – the basic phenomenon that the Danish philosopher Knud Ejler Løgstrup formulated as 'to venture out in the hope of being received'. In human relationships, we have a responsibility to respond to the other by addressing them instead of turning our back. This is especially the case when it comes to children.

In order to transform immediate feelings of joy and happiness – but also, of course, frustration and fear – into thinking, the emotions must be turned into signals and, in turn, symbols. This happens when a perception (an acknowledgement of something in the outside world) is separated from an action. Sensing and action are systematically linked early in the child's life when an outward-looking action (for example, a smile) immediately follows from experiencing something with the senses (for example, the mother's happy face). We know the phenomenon from adulthood, too, although it isn't always to our advantage if sensing and action are too closely linked. To give a very simple example illustrating the problem of a lack of thinking: if we are unable to think in a given situation or don't have time to do so, we may react violently to a provocation. Imagine, for example, somebody being accosted in a pub by another drinker and instinctively lashing out. The action isn't separated from the perception of the other but follows immediately from it.

Young children live in precisely such a state of immediacy. From time to time, adults do too – when slightly the worse for wear in the pub, for example. If, on the other hand, we manage to notice and acknowledge the emotional signal – 'oh my gosh, you're threatening, and it makes me scared/angry' – we can avoid acting in the moment, because the act of recognising the emotion effectively intervenes as a mediating influence. If we possess the language to understand the situation, we can, for example, ask the antagonist what they're doing. We may also have time to reflect on what we ought to do. An emotional signal intervenes as a link between perception and action and slows the process down. And that, basically, is what emotions and thoughts do: slow down the pace between sensing and action, so you have time to think.

In psychology, humans can have a mediated (or conveyed) relationship with reality via language and symbols. This is made possible by the distance we can establish, in the first instance, between our emotions and our impulses. Once we learn to attach linguistic concepts to emotions in situations, that distance becomes even greater, allowing even more time for reflection. As Dewey put it, thinking occurs in situations where you are stuck, where there is a conflict or where doubts arise. In cases like those, you need some kind of barrier that will make you stop and think, and emotions often play this role. In psychological terms, thinking is spurred on by 'speed bumps' on the road that force us to slow down.

Children learn to think because they have first learned to signal their emotions rather than act automatically. In this way, thinking becomes a kind of substitute action. We think something through – a possible future, for example – without acting it out in practice. We may then act if we think there is good reason to do so. Or not, if we think that's best. The point is also that children can only learn the necessary emotional distancing, and therefore the symbolisation that is a prerequisite for thinking, if they engage in a process of social interaction based on the transfer and acquisition of cultural practices. For example, children whose physiological needs are met but who are never acknowledged or interacted with – such as those discovered in the notorious orphanages in Romania after the fall of the Ceaușescu regime – may not learn how to participate in the emotional exchanges that are a precondition for developing the ability to think. They may not even learn how to speak or use concepts. They don't learn to see how their emotional signals are picked up by others, which means they don't acquire the necessary capacity for self-reflection. We can only learn to think for ourselves because we have learned to think along with others in emotional exchanges. Thinking stems from dialogue with others. That is where your *daimon* comes from. And it presupposes that others want to engage in dialogue with you.

Thinking as a higher mental function

The Russian psychologist Lev Vygotsky, who died in 1934, explained in great detail how both our emotional and social lives are crucial components in how human thinking develops. Despite dying young, he founded a research tradition called cultural-historical psychology, which formed the backdrop for much of modern developmental psychology. Hailed as a genius, Vygotsky was dubbed 'the Mozart of psychology'. He studied psychological functions such as thinking, memory, will and language use – not as static phenomena established once and for all, but as ongoing processes of development.[2] He also distinguished between lower and higher psychological functions,[3] stating that the former (for example, our basic sensory abilities and primary emotions) emerge during biological maturation, while the latter are cultural and develop in individuals through social activities. The development of thinking and other higher psychological functions occurs as a result of the individual mastering specific cultural tools. Here again tools should be understood in a broad sense that includes language. A simple example of a tool linked to the development of a psychological function is the knots on a string that certain pre-Colombian cultures in South America have used as an *aide-mémoire*.[4] The use of this tool was born of certain social

Where does thinking come from? 97

demands and challenges – specifically, keeping track of goods. A practice was, therefore, developed to help people remember. Once such a social practice exists, new generations adopt and perpetuate it. Built into this perspective is also an understanding of development: the individual's psychological life must be understood as a manifestation of socially and historically determined patterns of interaction inscribed in their mind. In other words, the individual's psyche reflects their life as part of society. At least, that is the case until the individual is fully formed and capable of thinking independently and expressing reasoned opinions. We develop psychologically as we master the practices on which our societies depend (agriculture, medicine, music, construction and much more). Thinking enables us to detach ourselves from the conditions from which we emerge. It is essential to authority and personal autonomy – the ability to take responsibility for the words and actions we bring to society.

Vygotsky asserted that any psychological function in child development occurs twice: first socially, between people, and then individually, 'inside' the child. To illustrate this, he analyses the development of the ability to point. Adults can easily point out objects, usually using their index finger. Such intentional movements are only possible because there is a background to the action not thematised by the action itself. In other words, the person observing the pointing understands that they're expected to look in the direction indicated by the index finger rather than the elbow – just one of many background conditions for the act of pointing. A child usually begins to understand pointing at around nine months old, once they've established what developmental psychologists call secondary intersubjectivity. This means that the communicating parties can all pay attention to something outside the communication process. Primary intersubjectivity concerns, for example, the exchange of shared emotional expressions (the 'proto-conversation'), whereas secondary intersubjectivity makes it possible to refer to phenomena external to the relationship. In other words, the conversation is about something other than the conversation. In fact, this is the fundamental function of language: to point at our shared world in such a manner that we are all able to talk about it in a way that every one of us understands the same thing.

Vygotsky observed that hand movements in young children are an (unsuccessful) attempt to grab objects. Children simply reach for objects that they find appealing for one reason or another. The predisposition to make such grasping movements is an innate part of the child's elementary psychological functions, which will mature during their early life. However, once the child's caregivers realise the meaning of the failed grasping movement, they will usually respond, often handing the child the object. Vygotsky contends that this movement gradually transforms from a grasping movement to a pointing one. The child discovers that they can use the movement not only to grasp things, but as a sign that is understood by others, and which often produces the desired result. Here, pointing is established as action, a meaningful movement, in a process Vygotsky calls 'internalisation'. The movement goes from being a reflex to being intentional. It's now about something other than itself – just like verbal language. This is in line with the earlier point, that an emotion (the desire to achieve something by grasping) becomes a signal (pointing), which in turn is fundamental to the ability to use language to point out objects ('Hand me the salt') and think more abstractly ('Is this much salt bad for me?'). Remember the formula from before: emotions in relationships produce language, which leads to thinking.

It is clear from Vygotsky's description of pointing that humans have a number of instinctive modes of reaction, including reaching for things and responding to the movements of others. These modes, like psychological functions, are elementary. To understand how they develop into thinking and other higher psychological functions, we must look at the meaning or significance they acquire. A pointing gesture, considered as a purely physical event, isn't meaningful in itself. It only becomes 'pointing' when the movement is perceived on the basis of a wider practice that transcends contexts and time and enables people to point out objects to one another. The movement is part of a system of cultural contexts. It is not legitimate to point at everything, for example. While you can point at the saltshaker, it would probably be socially inappropriate to point at somebody's big nose. While the pointing example may seem a little banal, it illustrates that even a seemingly simple gesture is part of a complex social choreography based on often implicit expectations and norms. As we gradually learn to understand the norms associated with a phenomenon such as pointing – and myriad other social practices – our ability to think develops. If we don't understand that we can point – and that the pointing finger is referring to something other than itself – we are unlikely to understand how verbal language can point out objects in the world. After all, the word 'cat' doesn't describe its own phonetic sound or the shape of its letters, but refers to soft, meowing, furry creatures. Once you master the use of this word, you can move on to more abstract discussion of, for example, whether dogs or cats are more adorable. Incidentally, neither dogs nor cats understand pointing – they just look at the finger, not what the finger is pointing at. If Vygotsky is right, it is precisely this shortcoming that explains why they are unable to acquire actual language or learn to think like humans.

Vygotsky's work was motivated by one question in particular: How to understand the origin of human beings' free actions and conscious behaviour?[5] As we have seen, the answer lies in the theory that people learn to use tools and language in social contexts, which – via thinking – give us a mediated relationship to the self. Language gives us a sense of distance from ourselves, which means that we can think in a reflective manner that takes into account not only the immediate present but also the past and future. This ability to distance ourselves from our impulses originates in our emotions. Once we also develop the ability to symbolise, thinking becomes possible. According to Vygotsky, humans can choose and act responsibly because they are not compelled to react in a knee-jerk manner. Instead, they use historically developed tools to modify their environments via signs and symbols, and in doing so structure their surroundings. The behaviourists are mostly correct to say that we respond to external stimuli, but they forget that we are also cultural beings with the ability to shape our experience. If you can't choose what to have for dinner when in the supermarket, a shopping list is useful. If you're distracted by all the notifications on your smartphone, turn them off so you're not constantly bombarded with beeps. We use tools to mediate our will and ability to think – our higher psychological functions. By acquiring social tools and language, we develop the higher functions of the psyche and, as we use them, we gain control over our actions. As such, thinking is closely linked to controlling our behaviour and deciding which stimuli to permit in our surroundings.

The natural history of thinking

How babies and children learn to think is one thing. How humanity developed this ability is another. Some evolutionary psychologists and linguists believe that there was a sudden genetic leap at some point in history, leading to an explosion in the ability to symbolise. This might explain the emergence of cave paintings around 20,000 years ago. Perhaps a kind of mental language module developed in the brain that gave *Homo sapiens* the capacity for language, which could explain why, despite having smaller brains and weaker bodies than Neanderthals, they coped better. According to Greenspan and Shanker, a more plausible explanation is a gradual transition to thinking via cultural transmission. Their theory is that it was through culture, not genes, that human thinking was made possible and has been perpetuated. As early humans began to externalise their activity through tools and images such as cave paintings, they gained the necessary distance from themselves that is a precondition for thinking. In other words, they gained the ability to pause and move beyond themselves in order to think. This process takes place via both the emotional interactions described above and via different kinds of tools and technologies.

According to the philosopher Hans Jonas, three such external technologies or characteristics distinguish humans, in an evolutionary sense, from other species. These are (1) *the tool*, (2) *the image* and (3) *the grave*.[6] All three of these have prehistoric origins and are culturally developed and handed down. But, according to Jonas, each enables a different form of thinking.

(1) The tool is not unique to humans. Other animals, especially higher primates, use tools for different purposes – chimpanzees pry termites out of nests with sticks, for example. However, crafted tools, from the flint axe to the fine instruments of the modern surgeon, enable a uniquely mediated relationship with the world. They allow us to intervene much more in the world (think of bulldozers or supertankers) and learn about its otherwise unknown properties (atomic microscopes or astronomical telescopes). According to Jonas, all of our thinking about natural science is very much a product of our tools. Our ability to manipulate nature is intimately linked to sciences such as physics and chemistry, which would be unthinkable without tools. We might assume that scientific knowledge precedes the development of tools, but the opposite is usually the case: the potential to intervene in the world and steer and control it leads to theoretical knowledge of what we want to control.

We don't begin with theoretical knowledge of fire and then develop the technology to start one. First, humans learned to light fires with the help of tools, and then (much later) to understand the science behind it. As Heidegger also pointed out in his analysis of our technological culture, the tool invites us to enter into an instrumental relationship with the world, one that reveals objects as standing reserves for human intentions. That is all well and good as long as it doesn't lead to an absolutist understanding of the world.

(2) If the natural sciences (and especially physics) originate from our tool-using nature, then it is little surprise that we use images to invoke our aesthetic abilities and sensibility. No one knows why ancient people began to decorate the walls of their caves. Was it connected with religious ceremonies or a way of teaching young hunters? Or was it closer in spirit to today's art museums – were the representations of bulls and deer intended to serve purely aesthetic purposes? What we do know is that the image reveals a different dimension of human thinking than the tool. It's not just about something instrumental but also about meaning. The image has a meaning that can be interpreted in a way that is disconnected from its utility value. Many animals are aesthetically beautiful, but their bodily decoration also serves an instrumental function (think of the peacock's tail, used to attract females). Humans, however, can paint, draw, model, sculpt, build and decorate their bodies and surroundings in many different ways. The fact that we can decorate by 'externalising' aesthetics via images, stories, music and other media can be the starting point for a different and more meaningful form of thinking than the one associated with tools.

(3) Finally, according to Jonas, the grave is crucial to our metaphysical ideas. Graves have been called the first form of literature because they invoke something that can't be

physically observed. They denote the presence of a human being whose life is over. This is symbolically marked, in one way or another, in virtually all cultures. Even more than the image, the grave reflects a contemplative thinking that transcends the concrete. In other words, marking the grave adds a symbolic layer to the world. It facilitates exactly the kind of dwelling or inhabiting the world that Heidegger wanted to see. As the poet Søren Ulrik Thomsen put it, a grave marks the place where the deceased is not. It becomes the site for a being-in-world that is not only immediate and sensed but is borne by symbolism and thinking. If you don't teach your children to have respect for the non-instrumental, they are unlikely to have respect for graves and other 'useless' things. And the price of this is that they won't be able to learn to think in the Heideggerian sense.

Tools, images and graves are, therefore, ancient external expressions of different aspects of human thinking. They can be both instrumental and have intrinsic value because they generate meaning. All three appeared very early in the history of *Homo sapiens* (and perhaps even earlier). As such, there is something of a chicken-or-egg dilemma associated with these artefacts' relationship to thinking: Was it thinking that led to tools, images and graves, or did these phenomena lead to thinking? Nobody knows, but they do exist and help pass thinking's potential down through the generations in the same way as the psychological patterns of interaction so necessary in childhood. Therefore, in natural, cultural and individual life stories, the ability to think emerges from a complex interweaving of emotions, language and cultural tools.

Thought experiment 6: Buridan's ass

Vygotsky has played a key role in this chapter, and as a psychologist, his tools were empirical observations rather than philosophical thoughts. However, at one point, he refers to Buridan's ass, a paradox from medieval philosophy. Vygotsky uses this old thought experiment to illustrate the importance of the human ability to use tools. So, while the problem has more of a 'solution' (at least according to Vygotsky) than the previous thought experiments cited, I present it because it goes some way to explain his important ideas about human psychology.[7] It is also quite amusing to imagine what human life would be like if we couldn't relate to ourselves through cultural tools.

In the experiment, you have to imagine that a hungry ass stands equally far from two piles of feed, which are precisely the same size and equally appetising. What makes the situation a thought experiment is that, in reality, one of the piles would probably be at least one cubic centimetre larger than the other, and the distance to the piles could never be exactly the same. But what does the animal do in the experiment? Nothing, according to the classic paradox. Confronted with two equally strong stimuli, it's unable to act and starves to death. It is pulled in both directions at the same time, with *precisely* the same force, and is paralysed. The ass is like a metal ball hovering at the exact centre of a perfect magnetic field.

So what would a human do in the ass's place? As we have seen, according to Vygotsky, the human being is able to choose and act because, unlike the ass, we don't just react automatically to stimuli – or in this case, we don't fail to react because the two stimuli are equally strong. Human beings are able, to varying degrees, to structure the stimuli they encounter using historically developed tools. For example, a person in the ass's situation might toss a coin, a practice developed precisely as a way of resolving this type of situation. We can introduce stimuli in the form of signs and symbols that have meaning for us and make a choice in that way. We can make 'heads' mean 'go right' and 'tails' mean 'go left'. Of course, these meanings are not intrinsic to the coin – they are something humans attribute to the world. As such, it's the use of the coin as a tool and the ability to use symbols that elevate us above our immediate impulses. And that's why we wouldn't starve to death. Or at least, that's how Vygotsky saw it.

*

The story of Buridan's ass is a simple one, but it may lead us to reflect on the degree to which our lives are determined by the stimuli to which we react – and how these stimuli could be reorganised if we were to think about them and relate to them consciously. If Vygotsky is right, there is rarely a direct path between thinking and action. Instead, since our behaviour is linked to the stimuli we encounter, the process is as follows: Thinking leads to the conscious arrangement of stimuli, which in turn leads to action. If you want to change something in your life, it is, of course, good to think about it but, after that, good behavioural design (as it is known these days) is much more important than mental strength or willpower. For example, if we are trying to work and we want to make sure we don't constantly succumb to the many temptations of modern life (social media, online media, a fridge full of food), it's important to cut ourselves off from temptation. This is much more effective than trying our hardest not to be tempted. We are smarter than Buridan's ass because our ability to think allows us to imagine ways of rearranging our surroundings to avoid temptation. And by changing our surroundings, we can ensure that they stimulate us in the ways that we want.

6
How to think

The previous chapters have addressed questions about the fundamental nature of thinking; the social obstacles to free, critical thought; thinking's connection to happiness and formation; and, finally, the emergence of thinking in human history. Along the way, I have placed particular emphasis on forms of thinking that have intrinsic value, and how thinking people can generate meaning by contemplating the eternal questions of life and death, personal identity and the just society. Hopefully, the philosophical thought experiments have been helpful and provided 'food for thought' – a phrase that underlines how thinking must have both content and substance. We don't just think out of the blue. We think *about* or *over* something that we have encountered, and which is bothering us – in other words, a mental stone in the shoe.

In this concluding chapter, I will look at *how* to think, and propose seven ways to bring a little more thoughtfulness into our lives.

Think with the world

In her book *The Extended Mind*, science writer Annie Murphy Paul describes many ways in which our thinking and knowledge depend on things outside our heads. If we want to improve our thinking, we need to pay attention to them. The idea of the 'extended' mind or psyche is a starting point for an increasing number of psychologists and cognitive scientists. It means that thinking isn't just internal but is linked to bodily, social and material conditions. People think through language, gestures, notes, databases, calculators and everything else outside their heads. The famous physicist Richard Feynman was once asked if his notes were a record of his daily work. 'No', Feynman replied, 'I did the actual work on paper.'[1] A scientist like Feynman doesn't fully formulate thoughts inside his head and only then communicate them in writing. Rather, part of the process of thinking takes place on the paper. This allows him to think slowly because it takes time to scribble things down, and his thoughts are made visible for him and others to read. In this way, he can retain the thoughts, relate to them, delete some, and revise others to develop them further. To write thoughts down is to externalise them – to situate them outside the head. In effect, to read words on paper is to read each other's thoughts. We can all learn something from this – especially if we think about how to create a world conducive to good thinking.

The philosopher Andy Clark is probably the best-known proponent of the 'externalist' view – that we think not only with our heads, but also with the world. He asserts that humans are 'natural-born cyborgs'. We use objects and assistive technologies to expand and refine our thought processes. Human thought processes can include everything from glasses that help us see more clearly to scientific instruments, books, diagrams, and so on. Clark's theory focuses on how people and environments are actively and mutually involved in these thought processes. He concludes that thinking doesn't take place in the head – at least not exclusively – but also in the world.

He supports this theory with a wealth of everyday examples. Just think of a simple notebook.[2] If a patient with early onset Alzheimer's copes with everyday life by jotting down relevant information in a notebook, it is, in effect, a replacement for the brainpower that previously helped them think and remember. But there's no reason to think the notebook isn't part of the person's psyche just because it's outside their skull. If someone asks the patient if they know how high Mount Everest is and the patient says yes but can only answer by consulting the notebook (which correctly says 29,032 feet), then we have no reason to deny that the person knew the height of Everest. The notebook plays the same role for this person as the 'inner memory' plays for someone whose brain functions in such a way that they can use it to recall the height of the mountain. A person who doesn't have Alzheimer's might at first have trouble remembering it and say, 'Wait . . . it's coming to me . . . ah yes, I've got it now: 29,032 feet!' It's correct to say that the person knew the height of Everest all along, just as it's correct to say that the patient, who has to look it up in the notebook to remember it, also knew the same fact.

Such reminders can be helpful for people who have problems with their brains in one way or another. Sometimes environmental factors can replace lost brainpower. However, it's relevant for all of us who want to think well and deeply to know that experts in thinking – whether scientists, philosophers, writers, etc. – can't be understood solely on the basis of their brainpower or from having practised for 10,000 hours, as is often suggested. According to Annie Murphy Paul, good thinkers are simply those who have managed to arrange their environment and resources outside their head – in the form of objects, places, other people, the body and its movements and emotions – in a way that enables deep and autonomous thought activity. This includes creating a fertile 'ecology of attention' which affords sufficient peace and neither too few nor too many stimulating factors. Matthew Crawford discusses the concept of 'ecology of attention' in his book *The World Beyond Your Head*. One of the things he says is that silence is as important for the ability to think as clean air is for breathing.[3] For most of us, it is a matter of creating good, quiet spaces for thoughtfulness.

Think with your body

It isn't just the world that's important for thinking. The body is, too. There are typical postures that signal thought activity – the classic example being Rodin's famous sculpture *The Thinker*. In many ways, however, it's misleading to believe that thinking necessarily requires the introverted, sedentary posture of Rodin's brooding figure. Much of Western philosophy and science has portrayed thinking as a 'cold' intellectual process that takes place entirely inside the skull and for which the rest of the body is irrelevant. It's true, of course, that all thinking involves the brain but that is different from the brain doing all the thinking – and it doesn't mean that the body and the outside world are unimportant. Ultimately, it's people who think, not their brains. The comedian Emo Philips once said, 'I used to think that the brain was the most wonderful organ in my body. Then I realised who was telling me this.'[4]

In recent years, various media outlets have reported numerous wild claims by neuroscientists that the brain thinks and feels this and that. But it doesn't. It's an organ that sends electrochemical signals around the circuitry of the body so that the person to whom the brain belongs is able to think and feel. These signals only become thoughts and feelings when they are part of the whole of a person's life – and the person, in turn, comprises the whole of the brain/body/psyche in relation to other people in their communities. The body is involved in thought processes in a multitude of different ways. In *The Extended Mind*, Paul summarises much of the research in recent decades that has shown the importance of the body for the way we think. Her thesis is that thinking not only takes place 'inside the head' but uses the whole body when the person is engaged in all kinds of processes.

For example, have you ever wondered why people gesticulate when they speak? It's because they're thinking with their arms and hands while they talk. One remarkable thing about speech is that we sometimes don't know what we want to say before we hear ourselves say it. We become aware of our thoughts at the same time as the people we're talking to. In that way, it is the Socratic *daimon* to which we listen when we speak, and which works through us. The trick is to remember to listen to it because many people just talk without listening to what they themselves are saying. We might call this thoughtless speech. It's common among politicians who've learned a lot of soundbites by rote, which they just reel off, regardless of the question asked. If, on the other hand, you think through speech, you become attentive to what you're saying and how others are receiving it. You can then frame what you say next based on what you just heard yourself say.

Gesticulating with the hands while speaking can be a way of structuring the content of what you say, so that you can almost see it in front of you and use it to orientate yourself. Gesticulating can also help you remember the correct words. In fact, studies show that when people are prevented from gesturing, they generally speak less fluently.[5] The next time you are giving a speech, teaching or engaging in conversation, try sitting still with your hands by your sides. The chances are that you will find it well-nigh impossible because it stops you thinking with your hands. Gesticulating was probably humanity's first language. Long before they learn to think via speech, infants learn to think by gesturing, pointing and waving. There is now evidence that throughout our lives, the ability to think continues to be linked to bodily movements, especially gestures, so one way to think better may be to use the gestures you know. Make full use of your body, arms and hands when you think. Let yourself be physically led and moved by your thoughts.

Think while moving

Annie Murphy Paul also refers to several great thinkers – including Nietzsche, Kierkegaard and Thoreau – who stressed walking as crucial to their thinking. The famous American philosopher and nature lover Thoreau claimed that he had to walk at least four hours every day in the great outdoors to stop himself from going mad. Moving around outdoors helped him think. This is also true of Kahneman, who we met in the very first pages of this book. He said that his best and most thoughtful work with his research partner Amos Tversky arose on their walks through the streets of Jerusalem or the hills of the California coast. We can think with the body in several ways, such as walking.

It is literally about letting your mind wander, whether you are engaging in quiet reflection or active conversation with others. For many people, fixing their visual attention on the landscape around them, rather than being expected to maintain constant and intense eye contact, is conducive to free and open thinking. To think with the body is also to think with arms, hands and speech. Gestures are important, as mentioned, as is listening to your own words. Of course, the most important thing is to listen to others – but it's almost as important to learn to listen to yourself. Given the sheer volume of anecdotal and scientific evidence about movement's importance for thought, it's strange we still consider thinking a sedentary activity. As mentioned earlier, I think best when walking in the countryside, running or cycling. That's when my *daimon* comes out to play. Perhaps one explanation is that all digital distractions are turned off. The body is allowed to be naturally present, the gaze wanders like the feet, the attention shifts, unforced, from the song of the birds to the movement of the leaves in the wind. Even though (or perhaps because) the body is in motion, our thoughts can dwell. This confirms the words of the philosopher Theodor Adorno: 'If the thought really yielded to the object, [...] the very objects would start talking under the lingering eye.'6 The Danish philosopher, Steen Nepper Larsen, who has often cited this line from Adorno, reminds us of the aspects of 'thatness', as he calls it. I, for one, am reminded of them when the movement of the body causes a thought to linger:

> *that* we are always already entrenched in the language, in the history, in the social and in our own bodies – and not least *that* we will die our own death and have not determined our own birth. In addition, *that* human beings as a species have emerged via evolution, i.e. we have become entrenched in nature, and *that* both as a species and as individuals, we deal with both internal and external nature.[7]

And *that* is something to ponder.

Think with books

Fran Lebowitz is a truly hilarious arch-New Yorker who came up with a slogan that all librarians, and thinking people in general, should love: 'Think before you speak, read before you think.' While funny, it is also highly apt, as I want to emphasise the prepositions that follow the word think. We think *about*, *over*, *through* or *on* something. We need content to fuel our thinking. In the culture of written language that has shaped European history for a couple of thousand years, nothing has been a greater source of content than books. Although we can think without being able to read, literature undeniably helps us to think. Thoreau, as mentioned, recommended four hours of walking a day, which is probably too much for most people, but I wonder whether or not most people could squeeze at least half an hour of book reading per day into even a busy life – or even a few minutes scribbling in a diary? As the philologist Irene Vallejo describes, in a fantastic work on the history of the book (called *Papyrus: The Invention of Books in the Ancient World* in English, but the more mysterious Spanish title, *El infinito en un junco*, literally translates as 'Eternity in a Reed'), it is through books and reading that we can think about the world, 'see words and think slowly about them, instead of just hearing them in the torrent of uttered speech'.[8] Writing is a way of slowing down the speed of thought so we can see our thoughts in front of us, relate to them, add, subtract and grow wiser.

Throughout this book, I have sought to explore the idea that thoughtfulness is linked to slowing down. Book readers choose their own pace. You can read slowly, read the same page several times, sit with a pencil and write notes in the margins (unless it's a library book). I was fortunate enough to inherit much of the library of my late mentor and PhD supervisor, Steinar Kvale. His books are full of underlining and notes in the margins. So when I read them today, they offer a window into the thinking of this influential academic. In principle, our thoughts can be fuelled by content from myriad forms of other media – films, TV series and music can certainly be thought-provoking too – but these have a temporal dimension, with a fixed speed determined by the director, musician or producer. They don't offer us, as viewers or listeners, the same opportunity to slow down and think at our own pace. I also enjoy poetry and have a particular fondness for very short poems that fit on a single page of a book, such that the letters almost form a miniature painting. I can repeatedly revisit poems like these (assuming they are good) to awaken my slumbering *daimon*.

Think with children

I have often found that some of the most imaginative and thoughtful conversations are those with children. Although children's thinking isn't necessarily logical and disciplined, they have an extraordinary knack for asking insightful questions. This is perhaps the most important ability to develop when cultivating your capacity for thoughtfulness. All parents are asked questions by their children they can't answer off pat: Where do dreams come from? What happens when you die? Why do we have schools, anyway? What was there before the Big Bang? Why do children have to do what adults say? Every time you talk to a child, you soon find yourself on thin ice after they simply ask 'why?' and 'how do you know?' a few times. Children are born philosophers. Not because they reel off educated answers, but because they take very little for granted and challenge all kinds of givens with 'why' questions. I once saw a cartoon encapsulating this: An adult admonishes a child, saying, 'Question everything!' The child answers: 'Why?'

It's tempting to dismiss children's relentless questioning and quickly end the conversation by answering: 'Just because!' However, as adults, we can also practise seeing children's impossible questions as invitations to the kind of thoughtfulness for which it is otherwise hard to find sufficient time and space. I suspect we get annoyed with children not just because it's difficult to answer their questions, but because we see their questions as a waste of time in an otherwise busy day. But they're not. On the contrary, it is enriching to take the time to engage with children's questions, to wonder along with them, and to challenge them to formulate their own answers and arrive at meaningful understandings from difficult questions.

Think in conversation

Perhaps the most fundamental characteristic of thinking is that, ultimately, it's based on conversation. Even solitary thinking, when immersed in your own speculation, is a kind of conversation. All thinking is dialogical. Thoughts come to you, and you respond. But in a certain sense, you don't know what the next input into the dialogue will be – even if you're just thinking to yourself. You surprise yourself when thinking, and that's both the mystery and the wonder of it. On the other hand, it isn't healthy to overthink things or become obsessed – but that's not the theme of this book.

It is also possible to think along with others in actual conversation. It sounds banal but what emerges can be greater than the sum of its parts. Real conversation isn't just a juxtaposition of two or more monologues. It's a dialogue in which all participants constantly adapt during the process. A conversation can take on a life of its own, such that it isn't led by the participants, it leads them – perhaps to insights and perspectives they couldn't possibly have imagined while thinking on their own somewhere. Conversation, assuming it's a real dialogue, is uncontrollable. You have to surrender to it and trust that it will take you safely forward, along with those with whom you are conversing. Like most other valuable activities, thinking doesn't thrive when excessively controlled. If we want to control it, we risk destroying it. You have to release your *daimon* to achieve *eudaimonia*.

Think with history

When you think and create meaning, you do so against the backdrop of your life story and the history of your society, language, nation, faith, ethics and art. The deeper your insight into the historical forces that shaped you, the better you can think. But it has long been unpopular to cultivate the historical perspective. For example, a few years ago, the Danish politician and former prime minister Lars Løkke Rasmussen said, 'We must go forward into the future!' On an instinctive level, this seems obvious – *of course*, we have to go forward into the future! It's absolutely necessary to take an interest in what lies ahead, especially when running a country. However, I actually think that the best way to do so is by looking backwards rather than forward. The future doesn't exist yet, so if we go forward and look ahead, we can only see what is immediately in front of us. The danger of this is that we end up living in an eternal now, arranging everything according to current impulses, which themselves may be quite fleeting and random. Thinking means looking beyond the present and imagining possible futures, but also looking back thoughtfully. The idea is to look behind us as we go into the future, so that we can see where we've been and map where we're going. By identifying how society was built, we can determine what is worth preserving and what needs to change.

Thinking with history might involve, for example, going to a museum and looking at artefacts behind glass. In a museum, the human being is, in a unique sense, removed from their everyday functions, just as the object is removed from its purpose. As discussed earlier, it is in this suspended state (in which all utility value is nullified) that formation takes place. Remember Iris Murdoch's point about 'thoughtful attention' as a kind of moral education. Letting your attention dwell on what has been is a form of training in basic thinking. If you read Swedish, you might want to check out museum researcher Sten Rentzhog's charming little book *Tänk i tid: Se frem ved at kaste dit blik tilbage* (Think in Time: Look Forward by Looking Back), a thorough and well-argued defence of the importance of historical knowledge.[9] Rentzhog's starting point is the same as this book's: that most people's thinking is trapped in the present. This reduces thinking to what is expedient in the moment, and it ultimately places us at the mercy of our random impulses. Only via thinking can we rise above the present, slow down time, travel with thought into the past and future, and perhaps – as Badiou would say – enjoy glimpses of infinity. Knowledge of history can help us do this because, by its very nature, history transcends the present. We should resist the faddish mantra of living in the moment. Only those who can't think do that. One of the great things about human beings is that we can live in time, not just in the present – because we can *think*.

Thought experiment 7: Your life

As we approach the end of the book, let's leave behind philosophical reflections on ethics, politics and personal identity and undertake a more personal and existential thought experiment instead, one inspired by research into people's life histories, which usually involve them imagining their life as a book and then answering questions like: What chapters will the book be divided into? How will the book begin? Which genre best characterises the book? How do you think it ends?

You can continue to ask yourself similar literary questions regarding your life-as-a-book. By its very nature, this is a thought experiment because our lives are *not* literally a book. But the idea is to encourage us to step back from the noise of the everyday and adopt a bird's-eye view of our life. If you like, grab a notebook and write a few pages about what your life would be like if it were a book – or a film, if you prefer.

If it's a film, pick out the highlights that would be in the trailer. Who would direct it? Who would play the lead? What would the soundtrack be like?

The purpose of the experiment is to show that it isn't just eternal philosophical questions that can stimulate thoughtfulness. Dwelling on your own life story can do it, too. If you are to understand yourself properly, it's not enough to know your personality traits or inner self. You also need to understand the life you live – and have lived – and the forces that shaped it. That is perhaps the most basic exercise in thoughtfulness.

*

Descartes' philosophical tenet from the 1600s is well known: 'I think, therefore I am.' But what does it mean to exist because we think? Of course, we still exist when we're not thinking – when making love, for example, or taking a nap. I don't think Descartes would deny that. And as these examples illustrate, we undoubtedly derive enjoyment and value from activities unrelated to thinking. But Descartes is right to say that we affirm our existence in a special way through thinking. When we think, we *know* we exist. We're not only conscious – we're conscious of being conscious. It is then that we are able to reflect on our lives, our relationships with our fellow human beings, and other ethical, political and existential concerns. It is the prerogative of humankind – and humankind alone – to make use of the faculty of thinking. Humans can be reflective, considerate and contemplative precisely because they are capable of this thoughtfulness. This is the source from which meaning, happiness and formation arise. But we need to practise thoughtfulness and create better conditions for thinking, particularly in a society that has focused for so long on efficiency over immersion, and utility over meaning.

Notes

Introduction

1 D. Kahneman, *Thinking, Fast and Slow*. New York: Farrar, Straus and Giroux, 2013.
2 L. Wittgenstein, *Philosophical Investigations*. Oxford: Basil Blackwell, 1953, p. 107.
3 M. Heidegger, *What is Called Thinking?* New York: Harper & Row, 1968, p. 28.
4 https://mindfulness.au.dk/kom-godt-i-gang/viden-om-mindfulness-og-compassion/#c128240.
5 Plato, *The Republic*, trans. Benjamin Jowett, Book II, 358d–361d, https://www.gutenberg.org/files/55201/55201-h/55201-h.htm

1 What do you think?

1 I. Murdoch, *Metaphysics as a Guide to Morals*. London: Chatto & Windus, 1992, p. 3.
2 A. M. Paul, *The Extended Mind: The Power of Thinking Outside the Brain*. New York: Houghton Mifflin Harcourt, 2021, p. 153.
3 P. M. S. Hacker, *The Intellectual Powers: A Study of Human Nature*. Oxford: Wiley Blackwell, 2013, p. 357.
4 I analysed Dewey's thinking in S. Brinkmann, *John Dewey – en introduktion*. Copenhagen: Hans Reitzels Forlag, 2006.
5 J. Dewey, *How We Think*. Lexington: D. C. Heath and Company, 1920, p. 9.
6 Dewey, *How We Think*, p. 139.

7 B. Schwartz, Science, scholarship, and intellectual virtues: A guide to what higher education should be like. *Journal of Moral Education*, 51, 2022, pp. 61–72.
8 P. Foot, The problem of abortion and the doctrine of double effect. *Oxford Review*, 5, 1967, pp. 5–15.
9 J. J. Thomson, The trolley problem. *The Yale Law Journal*, 94, 1985, pp. 1395–415.

2 Why has it become difficult to think?

1 Hartmut Rosa in particular has described this social acceleration, e.g. in H. Rosa, *Social Acceleration: A New Theory of Modernity*. New York: Columbia University Press, 2015.
2 https://www.cnbc.com/2019/09/22/heres-how-many-hours-american-workers-spend-on-email-each-day.html
3 S. Critchley, *The Faith of the Faithless*. London: Verso, 2012.
4 Heidegger, *What is Called Thinking?*, p. 20.
5 M. Heidegger, The question concerning technology (1954). In D. F. Krell (ed.), *Basic Writings: Martin Heidegger*. London: Routledge, 1993.
6 Heidegger, The question concerning technology, p. 318.
7 Heidegger, The question concerning technology, p. 322.
8 Heidegger, The question concerning technology, p. 323.
9 See for example S. Brinkmann, *Standpoints: 10 Old Ideas in a New World*. Polity Press: Cambridge, 2016.
10 See for example M. Coeckelbergh, *Introduction to Philosophy of Technology*. Oxford: Oxford University Press, 2020.
11 M. Heidegger, Building, dwelling, thinking (1951). In Krell (ed.), *Basic Writings*, p. 350.
12 H. Dreyfus, Heidegger on gaining a free relation to technology. In H. Dreyfus and M. Wrathall (eds.), *Heidegger Reexamined: Art, Poetry and Technology*. London: Routledge, 2002.
13 L. Zagzebski, *Virtues of the Mind: An Inquiry into the Nature of Virtue and the Ethical Foundations of Knowledge*. Cambridge: Cambridge University Press, 1996.

14 The following is based on S. Brinkmann, *Hvad er et menneske?* Copenhagen: Gyldendal, 2019.
15 B. Rogoff, *Apprenticeship in Thinking: Cognitive Development in Social Context*. Oxford: Oxford University Press, 1991.
16 M. Nussbaum, *Not for Profit: Why Democracies Need the Humanities*, 2nd edition. Princeton: Princeton University Press, 2012.
17 J. Rawls, *A Theory of Justice*. Oxford: Oxford University Press, 1972.
18 See, for example, R. Willig, *Kritikkens U-vending*. Copenhagen: Hans Reitzels Forlag, 2013.
19 C. B. Skov, *Kritisk tænkning*. Copenhagen: Gyldendal, 2020.
20 T. Chatfield, *How to Think: Your Essential Guide to Clear, Critical Thought*. London: SAGE, 2021.
21 J. Kruger and D. Dunning, Unskilled and unaware of it: How difficulties in recognizing one's own incompetence lead to inflated self-assessments. *Journal of Personality and Social Psychology*, 77, 1999, pp. 1121–34.

3 Happiness is a thoughtful life

1 A. Badiou, *Happiness*. London: Bloomsbury, 2018, p. 87.
2 Badiou, *Happiness*, p. 57.
3 Badiou, *Happiness*, p. 38.
4 Badiou, *Happiness*, p. 85.
5 Quoted from T. Zittoun, Wind of thinking. *Culture & Psychology* (in press).
6 K. O. Knausgård, *Spring*, trans. Ingvild Burkey. London: Harvill Secker, 2018. (I freely acknowledge having used the same quotation in an earlier book entitled *The Joy of Missing Out*. I take the liberty of recycling it here due to its strong lyrical quality.)
7 H. G. Frankfurt, *The Importance of What We Care About*. Cambridge: Cambridge University Press, 1998, p. 89.

8 Z. Hitz, *Lost in Thought: The Hidden Pleasures of an Intellectual Life*. Princeton: Princeton University Press, 2020, p. 185.
9 Hitz, *Lost in Thought*, p. 93.
10 My reading here is in line with Richard Rorty's in *Contingency, Irony, and Solidarity*. Cambridge: Cambridge University Press, 1989.
11 I. Murdoch, The sovereignty of good over other concepts (1967). In *Existentialists and Mystics: Writings on Philosophy and Literature*, ed. P. Conradi. London: Penguin, 1997.
12 Hitz, *Lost in Thought*, p. 53.
13 E. Tind, *Kvinden der samlede verden*. Copenhagen: Gyldendal, 2021.
14 Tind, *Kvinden der samlede verden*, pp. 59 and 71.
15 Tind, *Kvinden der samlede verden*, p. 417.
16 Quoted in T. Ingold, In praise of amateurs. *Ethnos*, 86, 2021, pp. 153–72, p. 155.
17 S. Turkle, *Reclaiming Conversation: The Power of Talk in a Digital Age*. London: Penguin, 2015, p. 62.
18 A. Bryson and G. MacKerron, Are you happy while you work? *The Economic Journal*, 127, 2017, pp. 106–25.
19 R. Nozick, *Anarchy, State, and Utopia*. New York: Basic Books, 1974.
20 For example in Brinkmann, *Standpoints*.

4 Thinking as formation

1 The following sections consist of a rewrite of my contribution to S. Brinkmann, T. Rømer and L. Tanggaard (eds.), *Sidste chance. Nye perspektiver på dannelse*. Aarhus: Klim, 2021.
2 I also wrote about this in S. Brinkmann, *The Joy of Missing Out: The Art of Self-Restraint in an Age of Excess*. Cambridge: Polity, 2019.
3 A. Ehrenberg, *Weariness of the Self: Diagnosing the History of Depression in the Contemporary Age*. Montreal: McGill-Queen's University Press, 2010.

4 H.-G. Gadamer, *Truth and Method*, 2nd revised edition. New York: Continuum, 2000, p. 10.
5 A. Reckwitz, *Society of Singularities*. Cambridge: Polity, 2020.
6 L. G. Hammershøj, *Selvdannelse og socialitet: Forsøg på en socialanalytisk samtidsdiagnose*. Copenhagen: Danmarks Pædagogiske Universitets Forlag, 2003.
7 S. Brinkmann, *Hvad er et menneske? En filosofisk dannelsesrejse*. Copenhagen: Gyldendal, 2019.
8 C. Kluckhohn and H. A. Murray, Personality formation: The determinants. In C. Kluckhohn, H. Murray and D. Schneider (eds.), *Personality in Nature, Society and Culture*. New York: Knopf, 1953.
9 S. A. Kierkegaard, *Either/Or Part II* (1843), trans. Howard V. Hong and Edna H. Hong. Princeton: Princeton University Press, 1987.
10 H. Arendt, *The Life of the Mind*. New York: Harcourt, 1997.
11 H. Arendt, *The Human Condition* (1958). Chicago: University of Chicago Press, 1998.
12 H. Arendt, *Eichmann in Jerusalem: A Report on the Banality of Evil* (1965). London: Penguin, 1994.
13 Arendt, *The Life of the Mind*, p. 107.
14 T. A. Rømer, *FAQ om dannelse*. Copenhagen: Hans Reitzels Forlag, 2019, p. 16.
15 Rømer, *FAQ om dannelse*, p. 16.
16 Arendt, *The Life of the Mind*.
17 Arendt, *The Life of the Mind*, p. 160.
18 Arendt, *The Life of the Mind*, p. 234.
19 Thus named in O. K. Pedersen, *Konkurrencestaten*. Copenhagen: Hans Reitzels Forlag, 2011.
20 Pedersen, *Konkurrencestaten*, p. 190.
21 Dreyfus, Heidegger on gaining a free relation to technology, pp. 163–74.
22 Arendt, *The Life of the Mind*, p. 404.
23 D. Parfit, *Reasons and Persons*. Oxford: Oxford University Press, 1984.

24 For example: https://www.vox.com/science-and-health/ 2017/1/3/14148208/derek-parfit-rip-obit.

5 Where does thinking come from?

1 S. Greenspan and S. Shanker, *The First Idea: How Symbols, Language, and Intelligence Evolved from Our Primate Ancestors to Modern Humans*. Cambridge, MA: Da Capo Press, 2004.
2 The following is expanded upon in S. Brinkmann, *Psyken – mellem synapser og samfund*. Aarhus: Aarhus Universitetsforlag, 2009.
3 L. S. Vygotsky, *Mind in Society: The Development of Higher Psychological Processes*. Cambridge, MA: Harvard University Press, 1978.
4 S. Chaiklin, *Kulturhistorisk psykologi*. In B. Karpatschof and B. Katzenelson (eds.), *Klassisk og moderne psykologisk teori*. Copenhagen: Hans Reitzels Forlag, 2007.
5 Chaiklin, *Kulturhistorisk psykologi*, p. 274.
6 J. Jonas, Tool, image, and grave: On what is beyond the animal in man. In *Mortality and Morality: A Search for the Good after Auschwitz*, ed. L. Vogel. Evanston, IL: Northwestern University Press, 1996, pp. 75–86.
7 L. S. Vygotsky, Research method. In *The Collected Works of L. S. Vygotsky, Volume 4*, ed. R. W. Rieber. New York: Plenum Press, 1997.

6 How to think

1 Paul, *The Extended Mind*, p. 158.
2 The following is based on my 2009 book *Psyken – mellem synapser og samfund* (The Psyche: Between Synapses and Society).
3 M. Crawford, *The World Beyond Your Head*. New York: Farrar, Straus and Giroux, 2015, p. 11.
4 Paul, *The Extended Mind*, p. 4.

5 Paul, *The Extended Mind*, p. 72.
6 Quoted from Steen Nepper Larsen, *Evalueringsfeber og evidensjagt – kritiske essays til forsvar for fagligheden*. Copenhagen: Samfundslitteratur, 2022, p. 67.
7 Larsen, *Evalueringsfeber og evidensjagt*, p. 80.
8 I. Vallejo, *Papyrus: The Invention of Books in the Ancient World*, trans. Charlotte Whittle. London: Hodder & Stoughton, 2022, p. 119.
9 S. Rentzhog, *Tänk i tid: Se framåt genom att blicka bakåt*. Stockholm: Carlsson Bokförlag, 2014.